THE ULTIMATE GRAD SCHOOL SURVIVAL GUIDE

GETTING IN · GETTING MONEY · EXAMS AND CLASSES · THE PROFS · THE THESIS / DISSERTATION

Lesli Mitchell

PETERSON'S
Princeton, New Jersey

Visit Peterson's Education Center on the Internet
(World Wide Web) at http://www.petersons.com

Copyright © 1996 by Lesli Mitchell

Library of Congress Cataloging-in-Publication Data
Mitchell, Lesli.
  The ultimate grad school survival guide / Lesli
    Mitchel.
        p. cm.
    Includes index.
    ISBN 1-56079-580-8
      1. Universities and colleges—United States—
Graduate work—Handbooks, manuals, etc.
2. Study skills—United States—Handbooks,
manuals, etc.   I. Title.
LB2371.4M58   1996
378.1'553—dc20   96-29360
                                               CIP

Editorial direction by Carol Hupping
Production supervision by Bernadette Boylan
Editing by Hugh O'Neill
Composition by Linda Williams
Creative direction by Linda Huber
Cover design by Greg Wozney
Interior design by Cynthia Boone

Printed in the United States of America

10 9 8 7 6 5 4 3 2 1

CONTENTS

ACKNOWLEDGMENTS

I am indebted to the students who participated in my Internet survey, as well as the administrators and faculty who contributed their expertise and experiences. With their help, this book became a universal classroom, with guest speakers from around the world.

In particular, I would like to thank Bernadette Boylan, Carol Hupping, and Jan Gallagher for their overwhelming support of this project and impressive editorial supervision; Robert Sattelmeyer and Sidney Petrovich for their excellent advice on preparing grant proposals; Patricia Bryan, whose nurturing influence has contributed to my success in more ways than I can count; Marie Mons for her financial aid suggestions; Margie Patterson and Matt Stinson, who never got tired of seeing me at the Interlibrary Loan Office; Cathy Brack for getting me through much more than just the writing of this book; Daniel Mytelka and Jennifer Sandberg for their input on the "day-in-the-life" of science students; and the students, faculty, and staff of Georgia State University's Department of English. Their comraderie, enthusiasm, and dedication both to the field and to graduate studies kept me motivated and inspired.

Finally, I would like to extend a heartfelt "thank you" to my family and friends, who never doubted that I could carry out such an ambitious project.

DEDICATION

*To my husband, Jeff Spruell, who didn't
know what he was getting himself into when he said,
"Yeah, that sounds like a great idea for a book . . .".*

READ ME FIRST!

The Undergraduate Myth: "Grad school is like undergrad, but harder."

Everybody thinks this—*until* they start grad school. Most new grad students wander around in a daze the first few weeks, thinking they have been transported to an alien (and hostile) planet. The truth is that grad school is nothing like undergrad—it *is* a different planet.

WHAT'S THE DIFFERENCE BETWEEN UNDERGRAD AND GRAD SCHOOL?

Leaving the nest. The most important aspect of graduate training in all its phases is the ability to work without direct supervision. In the academic spectrum you're more like an independent faculty member than a dependent student. You can't count on being nurtured by an indulgent academic parent; you're supposed to survive (and thrive) on your own. In grad school you'll decide on your course work, take charge of your classroom and discipline yourself to do research. In addition to these program-specific requirements, grad students must manage related aspects of grad school like financial resources.

Learning to specialize. One reason for this independence is the graduate emphasis on a particular specialty within the broader field. Grad students are expected to narrow down their interests in a field to a particular subject area. An English student doesn't just specialize in "literature"—he or she has a specialty area like "postcolonial American literature with an emphasis on noncanonical women's texts and cultural theory," or something equally complex. Go to the library one day and look up random titles in *Dissertation Abstracts*. The titles are usually at least three lines long, incredibly technical, and probably cover a topic you've never even

YOU MIGHT BE A GRAD STUDENT IF. . .

1. you find yourself explaining to children that you are in the 20th grade
2. you have ever brought a scholarly article to a bar
3. you can analyze the significance of appliances you cannot operate
4. you start referring to stories like *Snow White*, et.al.
5. you have more photocopy cards than credit cards
6. you actually have a preference between microfilm and microfiche
7. you find bibliographies of books more interesting than the actual text
8. you regard ibuprofen as a vitamin

Source: Excerpted from http://www.cs.virginia.edu/~bah6f/funnies/gradlies.html

A DIFFERENT SOCIAL SCENE

Because students are trained at the graduate level to specialize, not generalize, grad students don't (or can't) "mingle" very much. Unlike undergrads, grad students have to make an effort even within their departments to get to know one another.

One student may be working on clinical psychology and another on psychology foundations, so they speak different languages even though they're in the same department. It is rare, unfortunately, for psych, history, and physics grad students to get together for a couple of beers at the local pub.

heard of before. By the time grad students finish their training, they know more about a particular subject than anyone else in their department.

Playing the game. University departments are inherently political. The biggest shock for new grad students is recognizing that political alliances and maneuvering exist among the faculty. You probably never saw this behind-the-scenes activity as an undergraduate. The most successful students are those who understand and avoid political tensions without losing their intellectual curiosity or their enthusiasm for problem-solving.

"SO, WHAT DO GRAD STUDENTS *DO*, EXACTLY?"

Grad students in the arts and sciences start out their programs like undergrads. During the first one or two years, while making the transition to grad school, they take courses for credit and receive grades on their papers, computer programs, proposals, projects, and so on. They may take a few required courses, but they are basically expected to choose classes on their own.

Specialization. During this period, students begin thinking about an area of specialization within their field, a process which differs between the humanities and the sciences. In the humanities, students are allowed more freedom to choose their specialization based on their own interests.

I took English classes covering several periods and gradually developed an interest in eighteenth-century British literature. Students in history, foreign languages, philosophy, art history, and similar fields follow the same route, taking classes while looking for a particular area that sparks their interest.

Students in the sciences have less flexibility in choosing an area of specialization. While taking classes, they are required to work in a laboratory under the supervision of a faculty member, helping him or her carry out a specific research project. Within this more limited range of options, science students do have the flexibility to work with one faculty member rather than another, or to pick a research project related to the different projects going on.

The social sciences—psychology, sociology, political science, economics, anthropology—do a little of both:

they have more time than science students to choose a specialization, and may or may not do lab work as part of their training.

Learning the ropes. Taking classes exposes students to the "big guns" in their field. They learn which faculty members have contributed articles or books that have changed the direction of research in their academic field. They also learn about hot topics in their field—the cutting-edge research—which gives students an idea of what to publish so they don't perish. As students take classes, they get a better feel for the academic discipline as a whole. They learn about academic conferences, where faculty members and grad students present their ideas and studies on new research. All of this information helps students carve out an academic niche just for them, a particular area of specialization within the broader discipline.

Jumping through hoops. When the coursework is completed or almost completed, most students are required to take exams, both at the M.A./M.S. and Ph.D. levels, that demonstrate their proficiency in the field. These exams are usually written and/or oral, taken over the course of several days, and graded by a small committee of faculty members in the department. Students dread these—common euphemisms include "The Test From Hell," "The Inquisition," and "The Bloodbath"—and with good reason. Some schools use these tests to weed out less promising students, and study time can take anywhere from three months to two years. Students may be given an intensive reading list of books and articles from which the test questions are taken, or they may be given the questions in advance. They may even go into an exam and field questions at random. The nature of the exam varies tremendously from university to university and from discipline to discipline.

The big hoop: thesis/dissertation. With the qualifying examination out of the way, usually at the end of a student's second year, he or she is ready to move on to "research." For Master's students, research results in a thesis, usually a 50-page paper on a specific topic; for Ph.D. students the paper is referred to as a dissertation and can run 200 pages or longer.

I wish someone had tried to explain to me how huge the transition was going to be from undergrad to grad school. I was an honor student and had received lots of psychological pats on the back and encouragement. I'm glad for that, but I wish someone had pointed out to me beforehand that, in grad school, MANY PEOPLE had been undergraduate honor students!
—Holly, Ph.D., English

FROM STUDENT TO SCHOLAR

Students work on their theses or dissertations with very little supervision. This last "flaming hoop" of graduate training requires you to work and think independently. As you become more specialized in your graduate training, you will know more about your topic than even your adviser and committee members.

I wish somebody had explained that you weren't just going to be learning, but that you were going to be made a part of a professional community, that much of your work involved gaining recognition and meeting people.

—Hunter, Ph.D., History of Science

The course work and/or laboratory work helps students gain an understanding of their field and narrow down their interests to a particular topic. By the time they have completed the first two years of grad school, most students should have an idea of an "unsolved problem" in their field that they wish to tackle in their thesis/dissertation. Their research into this problem and the resulting thesis/dissertation is supposed to be original and make a significant contribution to the field. All this really means is that no other published research deals with this problem in the same way as the thesis/dissertation.

Most of the research that a humanities student conducts will be in the library, reading journals and books, and traveling to special libraries or archives to gather historical information. The student is making sure that a) the problem hasn't already been treated in the same way; and b) the sources can prove that his or her solution is not way off base.

In the sciences, the faculty member and lab assistants have done most of this preliminary research, and the student serves more or less as an apprentice for the faculty member. Science students work in the laboratory conducting experiments, track down library sources, and help write grant proposals for continued funding of the project. Science students use the information they get from this work in their theses/dissertations, usually concentrating on one aspect of the overall project.

The thesis/dissertation committee and adviser. The standards for a thesis are much less rigorous than for a dissertation. The process of writing a thesis may only take months, while a dissertation usually takes years to complete. To keep students from wandering in limbo during this process, a thesis/dissertation committee of three to five faculty members oversees the student's research and writing. Students may choose the (usually tenured) faculty members to form their committee. The student's adviser, also called the "chair" of the committee, is the principal member who guides the student through all phases of the thesis/dissertation. In the sciences the adviser is the faculty member in charge of the research project and lab for which the student works. The adviser interacts with other faculty members on the thesis/dissertation committee. Ideally, your adviser will intercede on your behalf if any conflict arises between other committee members about aspects of your work.

The adviser is the *single most important person* for a graduate student's development. A good adviser will offer expertise, help a student make contacts outside the university that may lead to potential job opportunities, support a student against hostile criticism, and turn a green post-baccalaureate into a seasoned academic professional. An adviser who does all of these things is called a "mentor." Unfortunately, such dedicated faculty are rare among advisers, and few will be able to meet all of these criteria. The tenure system does not reward faculty for their expertise as teachers or mentors, but rather for the number and prestige of their publications and the amount of outside funding they bring to the department.

Even students with an active and supportive adviser and committee will be working on their theses or dissertations with very little supervision. This last "flaming hoop" of graduate training requires that students work and think independently. Because the thesis or dissertation requires an "original contribution" to the field, a student will not have others that he or she can go to and discuss aspects of the research. As students become more specialized in their graduate training, they will know more about their topic than even their adviser and committee members.

The thesis/dissertation period of graduate school is the most difficult phase, and many students experience moments of doubt, frustration, isolation, and even panic with the lack of structure. Some fail to make it past this point, leaving school with an unrewarded designation: ABD—All But Dissertation. Other students thrive in this liberated environment and find their own research so intrinsically exciting that they don't need external sources of support to keep them motivated.

Working as a grad student. Along with working on the thesis/dissertation, students are usually required to teach as part of their financial assistance package. Departments typically award work-based financial aid in the form of a research assistantship (RA), working for a professor in the lab or the library, or a teaching assistantship (TA), teaching undergraduate classes.

I think it's important to know that graduate school is diverse. From going to a smaller college, I was used to having friends and fellow students of my own age and background. However, in grad school I found that I was a rarity in going straight from high school to college to grad school. Overall this has been a good thing—I've expanded my horizons and my groups of friends. At first, however, it was a challenge to fit in.

—Eric, Ph.D., Economics

I had no idea how isolating grad school was going to be. The community-oriented activities that are built into undergraduate programs are mostly absent in grad school. The isolation is compounded because 1) graduate work requires intensive library research, reading, writing, and other activities that do not involve interaction with others; and 2) specialization in the field reduces your ability to communicate with people outside your specialty.

—Ida, Ph.D., Modern Thought and Literature

Some students will begin teaching classes even before they've finished coursework. Once the coursework is finished, most students take on a heavier teaching load, usually two courses per quarter or semester. The time spent teaching classes may get in the way of a student's own research. After all, the research is self-directed, but the classes are scheduled and the grading has to be completed by specific deadlines.

Defending your thesis. Once the thesis/dissertation has been written and suggestions for revisions by the committee incorporated, the student reaches the last phase of their graduate career: oral defense of the thesis. "Thesis" in this sense refers not to the M.A. paper but to the principal argument of the student's paper, be it a thesis or dissertation. The student's committee will ask questions about his or her research, methods, references, and conclusions, looking for weak spots in the argument.

Grad students typically experience anxiety during this last phase, after all the work has been completed. But the committee doesn't want the student to fail. After all, they have supervised his or her work. It is extremely rare for a student to fail the oral defense.

Grad school is a job. Grad school is a career in itself. It's no joke: you *are* a professional student while you're working on a degree, and each step you take in school contributes more directly to your job prospects than an undergraduate degree. During school you will make contacts with other faculty members and students, focus research on marketable topics, attend conferences and publish your ideas, and generally strive to make yourself more visible in the academic community. Each phase of your training contributes to your reputation with students and faculty members in the department and outside the university.

Grad school is probably the longest on-the-job training program that exists! Are you ready for it?

FINDING THE RIGHT UNIVERSITY

CHAPTER 1

*I wish someone had told me before I started
that there are two types of graduate schools:
teaching schools and research schools. I ended
up at a research school when I really only
wanted a Ph.D. so that I could teach
undergrads. So basically, I goofed.*

—Elizabeth, Ph.D. student,
Computer Science and Engineering

MY OWN STORY

After working a few unchallenging postbaccalaureate years as a corporate and freelance writer, I decided to go to grad school with no other goal in mind than to return to a more satisfying academic life. Buoyed early on by an acceptance to Cambridge University (but, alas, without financial aid!), I naively assumed that any American university would be happy to have me.

Based on this assumption, I put only a minimal amount of research into selecting an American graduate program. My application strategies were a catalogue of "no-no's" for grad school admissions. I applied to universities based solely on rank or attractive location; I put off my GRE General and Subject Tests and ended up taking both on the same day; I sent a comparative literature writing sample to English departments, unaware that many schools consider these separate departments. I focused on my "love of literature" in my statement of purpose. And I never, ever asked anybody in the profession about my potential program choices. In retrospect, I was lucky to be admitted anywhere. This was a learning experience for me, one that this book will keep you from repeating!

WHO IS THE "AVERAGE" GRAD STUDENT?

There's no such thing. Grad students come from all walks of life and continue their studies for a variety of reasons. You may be a graduating senior who wants more education to secure a better job. You might be out of school but want to change your career, or just miss the challenge and variety of academic life. Or you may want an advanced degree to move up in your present job. Some returning students are older, coming back to school for the sheer pleasure of it after their children have gone off to college themselves. In this book you will find helpful hints from students that represent this diverse background—younger, older, minority, international—across all disciplines in the arts and sciences.

WHAT ARE THE ODDS?

Before you decide that graduate school is your choice, you should be aware of the status of graduate education in the arts and sciences. Universities are now using the same models for reform employed for many years in the private sector. Many schools are downsizing and restructuring their programs to cut expenses. Flagging government funding for education has impacted graduate studies most severely, meaning that lucrative fellowship programs and public university funding have been substantially curtailed or even eliminated. Many universities are offering faculty early retirement incentives and, rather than hiring more tenure-track faculty, have replaced them with contract labor, such as adjunct faculty or more graduate teaching assistants. This means fewer jobs for graduating doctoral students who want to stay in the academy.

In some cases universities have actually reduced the number of students admitted to graduate programs. This reduction is a responsible move by universities reacting to the current academic job market and decreased government funding. But it means an even smaller pool of admitted applicants. I know of one student who received his B.A. from a top 10 school, had an "A" average overall GPA, and great GRE scores. He applied to top 10 universities for graduate school. Not one school accepted him for admission despite his outstanding credentials. His situation may not be the norm, but you should be aware of the competition. Even second-tier schools that used to have less rigorous standards have become extremely competitive, and many of these schools are admitting students from top 10 universities. It's definitely a buyer's market! The table below shows the percent change in applicants by field from 1986–1994.

APPLICATIONS ARE UP, BUT ENROLLMENT STAYS THE SAME

In addition to cost-saving measures by the university, prospective students face other difficulties. The number of would-be graduate students has increased, resulting in fierce competition among graduate school applicants.

According to the Council of Graduate Schools, applications for all fields in the arts and sciences have increased since 1986. Graduate enrollment, however, has remained virtually the same.

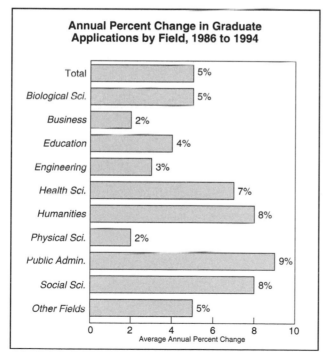

Source: Council of Graduate Schools.

DECIDING BETWEEN RESEARCH AND TEACHING SCHOOLS

Many students have found themselves at prestigious research universities only to realize later in their programs that they prefer teaching over academic research.

Community colleges, four-year colleges, and universities that place an emphasis on teaching may be skeptical of hiring a Ph.D. with a research focus, despite his or her graduation from a prestigious school. They assume that this type of candidate will leave as soon as an opportunity becomes available at a research-oriented institution.

HINT

If you're unsure about investing a full four to ten years in a Ph.D. program, you should find out if your prospective university offers a "terminal" master's program.

THINGS TO CONSIDER BEFORE YOU APPLY

RESEARCH OR TEACHING UNIVERSITY?

Most undergraduates are unsure about the difference between a research university and a teaching university. In terms of funding, research universities get the big money, from government grants to private endowments to corporate support. Research universities such as the Claremont Graduate School in California are graduate schools only—they have no undergraduates at all. The emphasis at these schools is on research and preparation for an academic research or laboratory environment. If you're pursuing a degree with the goal of teaching undergraduates at a college or university, a research school may not be the best choice for your career. Most schools combine the research and teaching components of graduate education, but many of the high-powered top universities will orient their students' education toward research-related academic pursuits.

Ranking sources may be misleading about the quality of research and teaching universities, so beware. The ranking of graduate programs is based, to a large extent, on the output of faculty research, measured by the amount of money granted to both individual faculty and the department. A top 10 ranked school may have a disappointing record of preparing students for careers in teaching. If teaching is your first love, be careful to choose a university that places the same emphasis on teaching regardless of its reputation for research in your field of study. I'll talk more about rankings later in this chapter.

M.A./M.S. OR PH.D.?

For working students or returning students with families a flexible program is a must. Although graduate locator guides may list program offerings of M.A./M.S. and Ph.D. degrees, some schools will not allow you to apply for only a master's degree. You are required to apply to a Ph.D. program and get your master's along the way. In addition, if you complete the M.A. or M.S.

degree and decide to go on for a Ph.D. at another institution, the doctoral program may take only a few transfer credits and require you to repeat the master's program. Students who pursue graduate education specifically to advance their careers may only need the two-year investment in a master's. And although you probably associate a "college" with only undergraduate education, many colleges offer master's degrees in various fields.

FULL-TIME OR PART-TIME?

Another component of a flexible degree program is the option to attend school full-time or part-time. Tenured faculty in traditional disciplines still tend to frown on students who attend school part-time, assuming that these students are not as committed to the profession as those pursuing a degree full-time. While this assumption is unrealistic given the increased number of older students with families, as well as the necessity of employment to meet costs, established faculty may have a bias toward full-time students.

TRADITIONAL OR INTERDISCIPLINARY PROGRAM?

One of the newest trends in graduate education is to pursue interdisciplinary research. Many universities are expanding their traditional programs to include degrees tailored to the specific research interests of the students. On the surface, an interdisciplinary program seems like an attractive choice for graduate studies. The admissions criteria for a nontraditional program may not be as rigorous as a traditional discipline and fewer students may be applying for admission. Obvious advantages are the potential for original research outside of a traditional focus and the ability to publish in academic journals across several fields. Potential students may believe their interdisciplinary knowledge and credentials will make them more attractive in the job market.

While the opportunities for research (and general intellectual challenge) of interdisciplinary study are undeniable, choosing an interdisciplinary program also has limitations. Government and other outside funding of newer disciplines has unfortunately lagged behind the academic enthusiasm for diversification. Students in fields related to the sciences, such as the history of science, are fortunate to have generous NSF support. Those in interdisciplinary fields in the humanities, however, such as cultural studies and specific ethnic studies, may discover that financial support is harder to come by.

Also, newer programs have not accumulated years of statistical information like job placement, time-to-degree, and percentage of students graduating that you need to select a good program. No doubt your cross-disciplinary research will be a valuable contribution to the profession as a whole, but you may still encounter difficulties finding a job. Because interdisciplinary professorships are still rare, you will be limited in applying for an academic position. If you decide instead to apply for a position in a traditional discipline, you will face competition with other graduates who have degrees tailored to that discipline.

WHICH FIELD?

If you're not sure exactly what graduate fields are out there, a good first step in choosing a graduate program is *Accounting to Zoology: Graduate Fields Defined*, edited by Amy J. Goldstein and published by Peterson's Guides. Although this book is no longer in print, you can still find it in most libraries. It offers explanations on a wide array of graduate disciplines, including nursing, business administration, and engineering. It's a good first step in matching your research interests with a particular field. Once you have an idea of your field of interest you'll want to make at least a preliminary decision on your area of specialization within that field. If you don't know what topic you'd like to pursue, reviewing information on schools can give you an idea of the kinds of research currently being funded.

RESEARCH STRATEGIES

The following is a list of criteria to consider before you go to the library and begin looking up specific information about schools and programs. Resources for finding this information are described later in the *Research Tools* section.

How much money will you get? A few sought-after graduate programs provide total financial aid to students upon acceptance. These schools may accept as few as ten students into their graduate programs, but once you're in you don't have to worry about funding and can focus completely on your studies. If you don't believe your credentials will get you into these competitive programs, you should find out what kind of support is offered at other universities. Combined with other information on financial aid, such information will give you a good idea of the financial support you can expect to receive. Financial support is usually not based on need. For more information about the types of aid available and how to apply, see Chapter 3.

For how long? In the student survey I conducted for this book, the most important factor for students in deciding among program acceptances was the amount of aid awarded and the number of years aid continued. This criterion also relates to the time-to-degree consideration below. Some students will be denied university support if they have been in the program longer than the specified time-to-degree requirements. You can still enroll, but you'll have to pay your own tuition and expenses. I know students in the humanities who balance less financial support with more teaching, but, as a result, cannot spend as much time on their dissertations as other students. Lack of adequate financial support is the number one cause of students failing to get past the ABD (All But Dissertation) status in getting a graduate degree.

What are the department's special interests? Another important consideration is the faculty and departmental research focus. Some of the students now enrolled in excellent programs targeted their applications at particular faculty members. This approach is very successful, particularly for students in the sciences. Not enough prospective students take the time to evaluate faculty interests and mold their applications to potential thesis/dissertation advisers. Keep in mind that the department as a whole may emphasize certain areas

For my research I made out a standard questionnaire with all of the items that were important to me.

I included such things as tuition cost, how much does the school cover, what are my expenses, what kinds of research facilities will be provided, will I have access to computers, what kind of computers are used, are there any new areas of research being developed, and about personal income, such as teaching/research assistantships, fellowships, scholarships, and any other financial assistance that may be available for graduate students like travel money for conferences or for conducting research.

—*Brian, Ph.D. student, Psychology*

of specialization, and it's important to know if your research interest is sufficiently represented in the department. If you're interested in a particular department you can review faculty publications to see if your research interests match.

Do their grads get jobs? Like targeting faculty and departmental specialties, this approach is often overlooked in deciding on a graduate program. A prestigious program that has a very low placement rate indicates a lack of emphasis on its graduate students. A solid placement record, on the other hand, means that a student's potential is not only valued in the department but also within the profession as a whole.

How long does it take to graduate? In the sciences, the average time to degree for a Ph.D. is six years, according to the Department of Education. In the humanities and social sciences this figure is even higher, between seven and a half years and ten years. Some departments are attempting to accelerate their students' time to degree, either by cutting off financial support after a designated number of years or by specifying in the course catalog that a degree *must* be completed within a certain time frame. If you plan on attending school part-time, you will need to know if the university will allow you to enroll for an unlimited period of time. Relatively short time to degree stats in a department can be a good sign for graduate students. They indicate that a department provides enough structure and faculty guidance to keep students out of dissertation purgatory.

Where do you want to live? In conducting the student survey, I was surprised to find so many students who had selected schools on the basis of location. Many students did not want to move out of state, others preferred either an urban or a rural environment to pursue their studies, and some applied to the same schools as their partners. I would recommend weighing location with other criteria. You could find yourself miserable at a school that's 5 minutes from home or 5 minutes from the beach, when instead you could have received better financial opportunities, emotional and intellectual support, and the growth experience of a new environment in another state (or even another country).

Before you cross out a school because the climate is too cold, check out the departmental climate.

What's the departmental climate? This information can only be provided by current students and faculty within the department. A faculty member at your undergrad institution who completed his or her dissertation at a particular school may not be aware of administrative changes or faculty replacements that can affect student morale. You need up-to-date, qualitative information on the departmental culture. Are the faculty and students collegial or competitive? Do faculty members take advantage of graduate students to further their own political agendas? Is the departmental climate a "chilly" one for women and minorities? Many of the students I surveyed wished that they had this information before they applied to schools. Some said that they would have gone elsewhere if they'd known how discouraging an environment they were entering. You don't have to make this mistake. Grad students are usually quite candid about the departmental climate and understand how important this question is to prospective students.

Any special facilities? Some schools receive grants to pursue special projects or to construct and maintain special facilities. These facilities are listed in most graduate school directories but you will have to look elsewhere to get information on funding. Before you decide on a school based on the opportunities provided through its facilities or projects, you will need to make sure that the funding will still be available during your graduate career.

Money from outside sources? Along with rank, this criterion marks the prestige of a department. You can find out about grants awarded to faculty, departments, and the university through several sources. Many times a faculty member or department may be involved in a special project funded by government, corporate, or other outside sources. Targeting your application at this research may result not only in your acceptance into the program but also in getting financial aid as a research assistant.

Rank? Taken by itself, this is the least reliable way to pick a school. The rank of a department will vary

EXAMPLES OF SPECIAL FACILITIES:

- State-of-the-art electronic or computer labs
- High-tech facilities for advanced biomedical or engineering research
- Special research centers such as a Women's Studies or Humanities Center
- Departments that maintain partnerships with local corporations, zoos, hospitals, observatories, special libraries, and the like.

depending on who's conducting the survey and what criteria are being measured. Ranking sources of universities and departments give you no idea of student satisfaction, the department's emphasis on grad student concerns, or the quality of graduate-level teaching. Looking up ranking sources should be one component of your research, but not the only step you take in applying. The department's prestige should not be ignored, particularly in a competitive academic job market, but you should weigh rank along with other factors in choosing a graduate program.

RESEARCH TOOLS

Now you're ready for the library. The resources outlined below will help you put together a list of attractive schools.

LIBRARY 101: PRINTED MATERIALS

Believe it or not, I know several graduate students who avoid the library! And even more were never trained to use the library as undergraduates and have learned their way around on their own. If there are a few years between your baccalaureate degree and your decision to return to school, you may not be familiar with some of the resources now available for graduate research. Here's a crash course on library research, which will help you get your feet wet for graduate-level research.

Directories. The two most popular graduate school directories are *Peterson's Guide to Graduate and Professional Programs* (soon to be available on disk) and the Educational Testing Service's *Directory of Graduate Programs*. Both can be found in the reference section of the library. They are divided into separate volumes for different fields such as "Humanities, Arts & Social Sciences" and "Natural Sciences." These reference sources are updated annually, so many schools will place older issues in the stacks. If you have a library card and don't want to spend 2 to 3 hours in the library browsing through the directories, you can check out earlier volumes to review at home. Once you've pared down your selections, a quick trip to the library's reference shelves is all you need to verify that no changes have been made in the most recent school entry.

The first volume of the Peterson's guide provides a helpful overview of graduate programs, including profiles of institutions, degrees offered by field, combined degree programs, and an in-depth essay on the process of applying to graduate school. In the individual volumes you will find basic information about specific fields, including:

- Application deadlines
- Entrance requirements
- Acceptance rate
- Average age and racial distribution of students
- Application fee
- Tuition and financial assistance
- Addresses and phone numbers for application information

In addition, some schools may include a one- to two-page description of a program that lists faculty names and their research interests. These faculty members descriptions can speed up your research, but keep in mind that some faculty will be listed who are no longer teaching or directing graduate students. Some may be on sabbatical, out of the country, retired, deceased, or otherwise inaccessible.

The *Directory of Graduate Programs*, published by the Educational Testing Service (ETS), is a complementary resource to the Peterson's guide, and you should use both to get comprehensive information on schools and programs. The ETS directory includes a handy worksheet in the front, not included in the Peterson's guide, that you can copy and use as a checklist for your research. It's divided into four sections that offer the following information:

- Program information by field (in the form of a chart)
- Institution information by state
- Narrative descriptions of programs by state
- Contact addresses

Talk to several professors about grad school before thinking about where to apply and what to apply to. Different disciplines are quite different in approach. Even the M.A./ Ph.D. concept is different in different disciplines.

In Molecular Biology and Chemistry, for example, the master's can be considered a minimal degree for those who don't have what it takes to get a Ph.D.; while in Ecology and Biology, a master's is an important degree to expand your network within the community and expand your contacts for getting a real job.

—Alison, Associate Professor, Botany and Plant Pathology

- Information about geographic location
- Student services
- Special research facilities
- Institutional resources
- Job placement of graduates

Ranking Sources. Ranking information can be found in several books and magazines. Most aspiring grad students are familiar with the *U.S News and World Report* special issue entitled "America's Best Graduate Schools," published annually in the Spring. The magazine interviews heads of graduate studies and department chairs as the basis for its ranking. The rankings are divided by field of study. This issue also includes interesting articles on current and emerging issues in graduate education.

Another ranking source is *The Gourman Report*, last updated in 1993, that provides a list of the top fifty schools covering different fields, versus the *U.S. News* list of the top twenty-five. In my opinion, *The Gourman Report* doesn't adequately explain its criteria for selection, and the rankings may vary widely compared to other sources.

You can supplement these sources with *The Educational Rankings Annual (ERA)*, found in the reference section of the library. This bibliographical source offers a comprehensive listing of all sorts of rankings in the field of higher education. The *ERA* will point you to books and periodicals that list specific information on educational rankings. You can look up your discipline alphabetically to see if any recent publications rank schools, departments, faculty, student attrition rates, financial aid, and so on, in your area of study. This is a great source to find unique information about a department.

If you still want more, you can turn to the indexes available for *The Chronicle of Higher Education*. Searching educational databases such as ERIC will let you know of *Chronicle* articles that rank departments and universities.

Grants and fellowships. For those willing to do the digging, the government documents section of the library is a gold mine. A reference librarian is essential for the uninitiated, however, to help you track down documents and make the most of your search. Contained in this area of the library are the annual reports of the National Science Foundation (NSF), National Endowment for the Humanities (NEH), National Endowment for the Arts (NEA), National Institutes of Health (NIH), National Institute of Mental Health (NIMH), and other acronyms. The annual reports provide information on government agency research grants to universities and departments, including the length, amount, and number of grants awarded. The NEH's annual report (document number NF3.1), for example, describes the nature of the project funded, the participating faculty, and the university to which the money was awarded. In addition, it lists fellowships awarded to graduate students and faculty and describes the nature of their research. The NSF's annual report (document number NS1.1) divides grants by state and lists the university, faculty, amount, and a short description of the research funded.

LIBRARY 102: DATABASES AND OTHER RESOURCES

Because databases on CD-ROM cost more than printed resources, libraries generally restrict access to enrolled students. If you're not currently enrolled, don't panic: Libraries duplicate the information in these databases with printed materials so you can still retrieve information the old-fashioned way, in reference books. For students who do have access to these resources, databases are a convenient resource to find publications by faculty or publications related to your research interests.

Finding profs. Database searching also helps you locate faculty in your area of interest. If, in conducting your research, you know that Dr. Erudite at Ivy League University specializes in early American colonial history, you can look up her recent publications on Historical Abstracts on Disc. From there you can get the bibliographical information and track down the articles to review.

The process works in reverse, too. If you want to pursue research in international monetary economics you can do a subject search of EconLit, find articles in that area, then see who's publishing them. After writing down a few names, it's only a short trip to the reference

DATABASES GALORE

An abundance of databases are out there: Art students can use the Art Index; biology students can use the Biological Abstracts on CD; computer science students can use the Computing Archive; literature students can use the MLA International Bibliography; psychology students can use PSYCLIT; and so on.

For every graduate field there exists a database with current publications, more than can be listed here.

One excellent Web site you can use to track down schools all over the globe is located at M.I.T.—http://www.mit.edu:8001/people/cdemello/univ.html.

This site provides an alphabetical listing of schools and links you to the schools' Web or Gopher sites. From there you can use on-line menus to direct you through the university's resources.

Another good Web site is Peterson's Education Center, located at http://www.petersons.com. The Peterson's site lets you apply to a graduate program on-line and offers general information about program applications.

The National Association of Graduate and Professional Students (NAGPS) offers a "Consumer Guide to Schools" written by graduate students. This is the only publication of its kind, providing inside information from students about the quality of their programs, realistic figures on housing costs and financial aid, campus safety, and more.

(continued)

department and the *National Faculty Directory* to find out where these professors are teaching. This directory is updated annually, but does not list phone numbers or E-mail addresses of faculty members.

Science and social science students are fortunate to have the Science Citation Index and the Social Sciences Citation Index. These databases tell you how many times faculty authors are cited in other publications. This is a great shortcut to learning about hot topics and prestigious faculty in your field. The indexes also include bibliographic information to track down publications for review.

University catalogs. University catalogs, alas, are generally only available on microfiche. Microfiche and microfilm are a real chore to use, but because most universities now charge for copies of their graduate catalogs, this may be the cheapest access you can get. If it's worth the trouble to save money on ordering catalogs from universities, a reference librarian can direct you to the microforms room where catalogs are stored. A more painless option for catalog searching is the Internet (see below). The catalogs are a good place to search once you've reviewed the Peterson's and ETS graduate school directories. School catalogs provide you with detailed information on degree requirements, faculty research specialties, and programs of study, and should help you significantly narrow your list of schools.

THE INTERNET

If you're not a currently enrolled student and don't have free Internet access through a university, investing in a service provider from home may be one of the best decisions you make in your graduate career. *Believe* the hype—because Internet evolved as an academic network, it puts the academic community at your fingertips. (I'll be offering all sorts of Internet tools throughout the book for use during the various stages of your graduate career.)

World Wide Web and Gopher. Most universities now have their own World Wide Web pages and Gopher sites.

These schools provide an abundance of electronic services, from on-line application processing to copies of the latest graduate student organization newsletter. Ambitious schools will make their graduate catalogs available, including department and program requirements and application specifics. Many schools have links to faculty home pages, which may include recent faculty publications (some include on-line copies of their papers), listings of current projects, projected teaching schedules, and their E-mail addresses and phone numbers. The campus wide graduate student organization (GSO) or departmental GSO may also have its own page. This page should include an E-mail address so you can network with students at a prospective school. Through this student network you can get detailed information about the departmental climate, prospective advisers, housing, the surrounding area—whatever you need to fill in your research gaps.

Discussion groups. And that's not all you can find on the Internet. You can also get involved in discussion groups—also called newsgroups, discussion lists, or listservs—in your field before you begin filling out applications. Individual newsgroups are too numerous to mention, but you can get a general list of academic discussion groups by doing a search on the Web. You can also use a Web browser like Netscape or your university's newsreader to follow newsgroup discussions without joining. The members of these groups will be your future colleagues and professors, and the electronic forum provides the opportunity to read and participate in worldwide discussions among students and faculty in your field. It's a great way to become indoctrinated into graduate-level discussions without being in the spotlight—if you're shy, you can just read the postings and learn about current topics in your area of interest.

On-line publications. And finally, students can review on-line journals. The humanities and social sciences have not gotten into on-line publishing as heavily as the sciences, but every field has, to some extent, begun publishing electronically. By doing a web search, you can find the locations of electronic journals, newsletters, and other academic resources. You can download and

Although the "Consumer Guide" currently lists only thirty schools, it is continually updated. You can reach the NAGPS WWW site at http://nagps.varesearch.com/NAGPS/nagps-hp.html.

The NAGPS site also contains other Internet resources of interest to grad students, such as the Information Exchange and Internet Library, links to university Web sites, and information about Alpha Epsilon Lambda, a graduate and professional student honor society.

DEPARTMENTAL POSTCARDS

Most departments provide postcards that you can use free of charge to request information directly from schools.

You can write to schools for information that fills in gaps from your other research, such as placement information, faculty research, the departmental research emphasis, a graduate catalog (if free), and applications for admission and financial aid.

The postcards save you money on long-distance charges, and you can call later on if you need more specific information.

read journals at your leisure at home to see who's publishing and what topics are hot in your field.

YOUR UNDERGRADUATE INSTITUTION

If you're still an undergraduate or have maintained close contact with professors from college, you can talk with them about the pros and cons of your school choices. If you're not sure yet of your research specialization within a field, ask several professors with different specialties for advice. You can also ask the department's graduate director about the details of admissions and program requirements. If your department has a graduate student organization, you can talk with these students about programs. Grad students always have friends at other schools, and they may give you phone numbers or E-mail addresses for students at the schools in which you're interested.

CAREER COUNSELING CENTER

At most schools you can use the career counseling center's services if you are currently enrolled or are an alumnus/alumna. A center's resources vary tremendously in scope from school to school. Some maintain current graduate catalogs from universities around the world, sparing you the ordeal of microfiche. Others gear their center toward employment and have virtually no resources on graduate school. But it's definitely worth checking out. A diligent center will provide searchable databases on graduate programs or financial aid, allowing you to search schools by various criteria such as location, competitiveness, and so on. I used one database to search for outside financial aid sources and was disappointed with its results; it contained an abundance of entries restricted to undergraduates or other credentials unrelated to graduate studies. On the plus side, you can print out your search results and review them at length to decide if you need more information.

PARING DOWN YOUR SCHOOL LIST

With all of this information in hand, you should be able to narrow down your list of schools. Most guidelines for graduate admissions recommend that you apply to no more than ten schools because of the time spent on applications and expensive application fees. If you've got the time and money, however, I say go for it—apply to as many schools as you want. The research should let you know which schools are realistic. When I went through this process again, applying to Ph.D. programs, I chose a slightly different approach to the "spray and pray" method I used with my M.A. applications. My school information soon became so unwieldy that I narrowed my school choices as soon as I could. My strategy was to pare down my list to five schools and then spend the rest of my time doing *serious* networking. By the time these schools received my applications, I had spoken with or E-mailed faculty, grad association students, students studying in my area under advisers I was interested in, and departmental administrative assistants.

I initially planned to eliminate long-shot schools to save effort and money. That is, until a friend of mine at Columbia told me that schools with long-standing reputations have less to prove and can afford to take in a few promising "dark horse" candidates. Up-and-coming schools, on the other hand, may be seeking students with B.A. or B.S. degrees from top 10 schools to increase their departments' prestige. I recommend that you go ahead and include a couple of long-shots in your choices. Once you've made your selections, you're ready to tackle the admissions process, which we'll look at next.

ADMISSIONS: GETTING IN

For my application essay I was mushy and sort of holistic and wish I hadn't been. Listening to department members and reading some grad apps since then I've found that profs mostly want you to have some idea of what you're going to do. They don't care about wanting to change the world through criticism or teach impressionable young minds.

—Denise, Ph.D student, History

When I began interviewing admissions officers and faculty, my intention was to put together a standard ranking of credentials: "Grades are the most important for admissions, then GRE scores, then the application essay," and so on.

But I'm sorry to say that it didn't work out that way. Each admissions officer and faculty member I interviewed ranked these criteria differently. Each school, and indeed each department, takes its own view about which of these are most important in making a determination. Overall, the top five credentials, in no particular order, are these:

- Academic achievements/experience
- GRE scores
- Recommendations
- Statement of purpose (the application essay)
- Undergraduate GPA (major and cumulative)

Although this may be a bitter pill to swallow if you are weak in any of these areas, your best assurance of getting accepted to different schools is to be strong in every aspect of the application. You cannot call the department's admissions committee and ask them how they weigh application criteria, although it would be great if you could! If you know students at a particular school, they may be able to give you some input about the selections process when they applied—they may even offer you copies of their applications. A few programs allow graduate students to participate in the admissions process, which means that the students can tell you more specifically what the department is looking for. Otherwise, though, admissions is a crapshoot, especially in cases where a committee must choose ten candidates from 800 applications! But you can work to improve your chances for admission, especially in preparing for your statement of purpose, GRE exams, and campus interview.

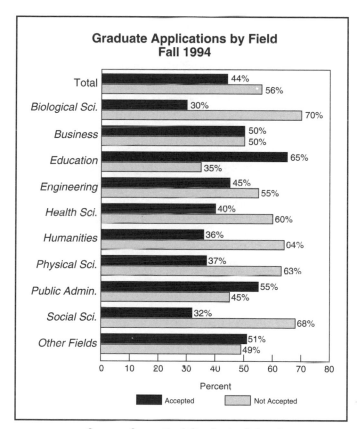

Source: Council of Graduate Schools

FOR SUCCESS:

1. Have clearly defined objectives and purpose for attending grad school.

2. Be motivated to do things on your own instead of relying too much on your academic adviser.

3. Plan your program early with faculty members who have an interest in your program and want to help you succeed in grad school.

4. Make sure you take care of business early in your graduate program. Getting off to a good start academically can build your confidence.

—*Kirk A. Swortzel, Graduate Administrative Associate, The Ohio State University*

ROUTING YOUR
APPLICATION

Graduate School
↓
Department
↓
Graduate Studies Office
↓
Graduate Director and
Admissions Committee
↓
Decision

VARIATIONS IN THE APPLICATION PROCESS

Unlike college, the procedures for applying to grad school are not standardized. Schools may request that you send all of your application materials to the graduate school, or, more likely, you will send parts of the application to the graduate school and other parts directly to the graduate studies office in the department. Because these procedures vary so much, keeping track of your application procedures for each school is the most important part of applying.

WHO EVALUATES YOUR APPLICATION?

When you applied to college, the admissions office determined whether or not you were accepted as an undergraduate. Not so at the graduate level. The graduate admissions office is an administrative branch of the graduate school of arts and sciences. You will call the graduate school to request an application, specifying the department and program (i.e., M.A./M.S. or Ph.D.) to which you're applying. All the graduate school does is review your application to make sure it is complete. Then the graduate school will forward all of your materials to the department for consideration.

Thus, you are not applying to "graduate school" as such—you're applying to an admissions committee made up of several faculty members within the department. The graduate studies office of the department also handles the administrative procedures of your application much like the graduate school does. This departmental office ensures that your application is complete, and once your application has been forwarded to the graduate studies office, you must call them to verify that all materials have been received. The graduate director of the department, along with an admissions committee of several faculty members, will then review your application. Based on the recommendation of the admissions committee and the graduate director, the department will accept or reject your application. The whole process can get a bit confusing!

APPLICATION TIME LINE

Because the applications process is so complex, planning out a schedule in advance helps you keep up with all of your materials and stay on target for your deadlines. The following chart provides a time line for getting application materials together based on a January 15 deadline for schools to receive your application.

FEBRUARY	MARCH	APRIL
• GRE General registration • GRE General preparation	• Continue GRE General preparation	• GRE General Test

MAY/JUNE/JULY	AUGUST	SEPTEMBER
• Library research on schools • Networking with students and faculty at targeted schools	• GRE Subject registration • GRE Subject preparation • Narrow down school list • Begin requesting applications	• Continue GRE Subject Test preparation • Request recommendation letters from faculty and/or employers

OCTOBER	NOVEMBER	DECEMBER
• GRE Subject Test • Request undergraduate transcripts • Begin polishing up writing/work samples or portfolio, if required	• Begin statement of purpose • Campus visits to schools, if desired • Collect all recommendation letters	• Finish statement of purpose • Copy and mail apps by December 15

FEBRUARY/MARCH/APRIL

Taking the GREs. Anna's horror story: The dreaded day has arrived. Anna was so busy with her schoolwork that she waited until the night before to begin looking over sample questions, forgot about getting her admissions photo taken, and was assigned a test site by ETS at a school she'd never visited before. Now she's rushing around at the last minute, calling Kinko's to see if she can get a photo made, calling the school for directions and the location of the classroom, and she can't remember where she put the GRE admissions ticket!

It's easy to forget some of the details about the GRE, especially if you have other work that requires immediate attention. Registering for the GRE is just the first step, and you shouldn't wait until the last minute to take care of the other details.

Scheduling the test. I took my GRE General and Subject Tests on the same day. Unless you're a masochist, I don't recommend this strategy. I had no idea how drained I would be in the afternoon, but by then I was in the middle of my Subject Test. The GRE

MODIFIED GRE TIME LINE

If you will take your GREs in October and December, here is a modified time line:

July
Register for GRE General Test
GRE General preparation

August/September
Continue GRE General preparation

October
GRE General Test
Register for GRE Subject Test
Begin GRE Subject preparation

November
Continue GRE Subject preparation

December
GRE Subject Test

Assuming that the abilities of the student have been established, a student's success will be affected by the congruence of his or her interest with supervising faculty members. The student should observe faculty members' ways of working and model those most conducive to academic success.

—*Daniel D. Blaine, Professor of Educational Psychology, University of Hawaii at Manoa*

General takes about 4 hours or more, including time to go over instructions and the 10-minute break, and my Subject Test took about 3 hours. I was able to have lunch in between, which I thought would be enough time to rest and gear up for the Subject in the afternoon. It wasn't. I completely lost my concentration by about question 100, and it never came back.

Other students have made the same mistake, assuming because the General is scheduled in the morning and the Subject in the afternoon that students are expected to take them together. Scheduling these tests should be your first concern in applying, even before you start requesting applications. Some programs will accept scores as late as the December test date, but this is not standard. You might be cutting it too close. Call the schools and ask them what is the latest acceptable test date for the application. Schedule accordingly.

Score reporting. *A word of caution:* remember that the registration form only allows scores to be reported to *four* schools. If you're applying to more than four schools, you will need to fill out the "Additional Score Report Request Form." Don't forget about this or your scores to other schools will be delayed. Fill it out when you fill out your registration form, and make copies of it if you have more schools to add than will fit on the form.

Test site. In addition, there are other preparations to make. Because the number of GRE test-takers has jumped in the last couple of years, you will need to send in the registration form much earlier than the deadline to get your first- or second-choice test center. I sent my form a month in advance and was still assigned a school 100 miles away from home. Some of my friends didn't get a space at all. If you end up at a school that's a long way from home, consider staying overnight in a hotel close to the campus so you won't be exhausted from driving to the school. Also, if it's a long drive, you can't be sure there won't be a delay on the highway.

General Test prep. This test is much easier to ace than the Subject. You can cram the vocabulary portion, and the quantitative section doesn't go beyond tenth-grade math (alas, many of us still struggle with it—how long has it been since you used the Pythagorean theorem?). Also, the analytical section—anything but a test of your analytical abilities!—follows patterns you can recognize by working a lot of sample problems.

Fortunately, too, there are several guides and classes available to help you prepare for this test. So many, in fact, that you may want a little guidance deciding which method of preparation is best for you.

Study guides. Students who did well on their test recommended two study guides over the rest: *Practicing to Take the GRE General Test*, published by the Educational Testing Service (ETS) and *Cracking the GRE*, from Princeton Review. ETS offers the best choice of sample questions because the guide includes the actual tests used in previous years. Don't be fooled by other study guides that include sample test questions. The actual tests are copyrighted by ETS and only ETS can publish the real test questions.

Cracking the GRE is an excellent supplement to the ETS guide because it offers test-taking strategies. Keep in mind with the GRE that you are NOT being tested on your reading comprehension, mathematical aptitude, or logic skills. You are being tested on how well you take tests—how quickly you can skim through irrelevant material to find important points and how well you can eliminate false answer choices. Particularly in the math questions, they're dozens of shortcuts and giveaways if you know what to look for. The Princeton Review guide is excellent for providing you with shortcuts so you don't have to actually work out the math problems (you're not supposed to work out the math—if you did there wouldn't be enough time to complete the sections). *Cracking the GRE* can also help you with reading comprehension questions, offering words and phrases to look for that will show up in test questions. It will also help you with general test-taking strategy, timing, eliminating answers, and relaxing during the test.

Prep courses. Because I hadn't had a math class in ten years, I took a Kaplan GRE prep course to refresh my memory of mathematical operations. Like me, some of you probably learn material better in the classroom than from a book, or may prefer the regularity of a class schedule to keep up your studying if you're busy with work, other classes, or family responsibilities. The Kaplan classes, like other professional prep courses, are well-structured and I benefitted enormously from them,

If you like the classroom environment but don't want to spend the money on a professional course, you still have options. The career placement office at many universities offers prep courses for the GRE, sometimes broken down into courses just for verbal, quantitative, or analytical prep, at a substantially lower cost than companies like Kaplan and Princeton Review. Sometimes you can take a prep class for as little as $50, a course that's well worth the investment if your score lands you a university fellowship.

THE CAT: NO GOING BACK

The computer asks for confirmation of your answer choice, doubling the time it takes to answer a question. In addition, once you've answered a problem you can't go back to your answer choice. If you think you got a question wrong, there's no fixing it—what's done is done. This inability to change your answers makes many students uncomfortable.

not only in terms of the material we covered but also in building the psychological confidence I needed on test day.

But these professional courses are not for everyone. The courses are very expensive, which is more understandable if you're pursuing an advanced degree in business, law, or medicine. For those students, there's a lot riding on test scores, and the payoff in future earnings will be substantial if the scores get them into Harvard or Johns Hopkins. For the arts and sciences, however, the payoff from a course that costs from $500 to $1,000 is less clear, and many would-be grad students are not willing to invest that kind of money.

GRE CAT. The computerized version of the GRE is still in its infancy at the writing of this book, but to date the feedback has been less than positive. The test has good intentions—CAT, or Computer Adaptive Testing, has been proven to be a better indicator of student performance than a standardized test. Instead of offering the same questions for all test-takers, the computer selects your particular set of questions based on your answer choices. If you answer the first question correctly, the computer will select a more difficult question for you. If you get a question wrong, your next question will be the same level of difficulty. In this way, each test is individual, "adapted" to the student's ability. In addition, you don't have to wait for national test dates to take the CAT. You can take it any day except Sunday at any of the test centers in your area, and you will get your score immediately, rather than having to wait six weeks for your score to be processed by ETS.

Sounds great, right? Except there are a few problems. The first, for students, is the cost. Taking the CAT costs almost double the paper-and-pencil tests. And students who have taken the test don't like the computerized format very much, despite being comfortable with computers in general. Here are a few of their complaints:

Timing strategies. For students taking paper exams, there is a certain comfort in being able to assess all of the questions at once and plan an attack. The computerized version doesn't allow for this strategy—you can't "see" the whole test because the computer generates it as you go. You can't use the timing strategy of paper-and-pencil tests in which you skip harder questions and answer the easiest questions first to build your confidence.

Formatting. The formatting of the reading comprehension section on the screen is less than ideal. The bulk of the screen is filled up with the question, allowing little room for the reading selection. Also, there's no way to fit the entire reading comp section on one screen, so you are continually scrolling up and down looking for important points. For many students this resulted in wasting precious minutes, versus the paper test in which the whole reading passage is right in front of you. Keep all of this in mind if you decide to take the CAT. Even students who have used computers for years said they lost time getting accustomed to the computer's formatting, and all said afterward they would have preferred the paper test.

A final word about the GRE. Some students have trouble with the test because they lose their concentration, to the point of getting angry at the questions. Watch out if your mind wanders from the questions themselves to thinking about the test as a whole. Negative thinking won't help you—don't get self-righteous by saying to yourself, "Jeez, these are stupid questions. Who cares if X cannot be seated by Y?" or "This is NOT a test of my abilities—this a test on test-taking!" or "Basing my admissions on a one-day test is insane! How does this show how I'll succeed in grad school?" If these kinds of responses occur to you in the middle of the test, try to get past them and get back to the question at hand. You will not be the only student to have a moment or two of frustration, especially if you're working on a tough problem.

My advice is to try to take the test seriously and save the complaining for afterward. Complaints about the GRE and how it's used to measure student success are manifold, but so far, it's the only game in town. Don't wander mentally outside the test—stay on the inside, focus on the questions. If you get frustrated close your eyes and take a couple of deep breaths. Then get back to work. You'll thank me for this later!

MAY/JUNE

See Chapter 1, "Finding the Right University," on researching and networking schools.

JULY

Subject test prep. Subject tests are slippery, but you can better your chances on them by supplementing your undergraduate course work with some review and new reading. Every subject test is radically different, but generally students prepare two ways: the ETS prep guide, which contains past Subject Tests, and reviewing intro-level textbooks that cover material you haven't had in classes. When you receive your admissions ticket from ETS, there will be a booklet that outlines the distribution of test questions—what percent of the questions cover which topics—that you can use as a guideline for studying. However, I found that, having taken the Literature in English test twice, this distribution was less than accurate. For me it was like taking two completely different tests. The surest bet is to try to know at least a little bit about everything. And yes, it will take time.

Mimic the test environment. If you use the ETS guide, you can take the first practice test however you like, just to get a feel for the questions. When you're ready to take a real practice test, take it on campus in an empty room (this also applies to GRE General Test preparation, if you decide to study for it on your own).

Make sure that you've eaten something before the practice test, as you would for the real test—don't fill up on just coffee or you'll be hungry and anxious. And dress comfortably. I wore sweats and even took my shoes off so I could cross my legs in the chair, the same as when I'm studying at home. This made me feel 100 percent more comfortable—almost like taking the test at home.

By taking the tests in a similar testing environment, you will not only be more prepared for the real thing, but your score on the practice tests will be a more accurate predictor of your score on test day.

How are test scores evaluated by the admissions committee? Most students I interviewed were pleased with their General scores, but almost no one was happy with their Subject scores, no matter how hard they studied. A word of encouragement: if your Subject comes back with a less than stellar score, don't take it too hard. It's extremely difficult to design a Subject Test that adequately covers material from an entire field. Invariably the test will concentrate on some area in which you're weak. Admissions committees know that Subject Tests have their pitfalls. In fact, many schools regard this test as a checklist item and will only be concerned if your score is below average. You can tell by looking at the percentile distribution of scores that even answering 75 percent of the test correctly—a "C" on any other test—puts you near the top. For both the General and Subject Tests, admissions committees look at the percentile rankings, not your numerical score. The GRE scores count the most if you're applying for a university-wide fellowship. University administrators must use standardized criteria, such as GRE scores and GPA, so they can compare students across disciplines.

AUGUST

At this point you should have your school list pared down from your research. Now you're ready to begin requesting applications.

Organizing your application materials. As application materials begin to arrive, make file folders for each school and write the deadline across the front. You will be tempted to start all kinds of lists—lists of phone numbers of schools, of application materials required for each school, of faculty in the programs—but my advice is to keep all the information pertaining to each school in a single folder. If you try to consolidate information into lists, you have several lists to keep track of, and almost instantly the material becomes unwieldy and disorganized.

Plan to send everything together. Even though schools may request that you send materials such as transcripts or recommendations directly to the graduate school or to the department, I would suggest that you collect ALL of the application materials yourself. This will save you the headache of calling schools individually and making sure everything has been received. If

ORGANIZATION TIP

Get a notebook and start a page for each school with information that you will need at your fingertips. The following information will be helpful to have close at hand:

- **Phone number of Graduate Studies Office/name of graduate director**
- **Graduate school telephone number and address**
- **Deadline for applying**
- **List of recommenders for each school**
- **Checklist of required materials, number of copies needed, and where to send them. Below is a sample:**

❑ **GRE General/Subject (2 copies—1 sent to graduate school, 1 to department)**

❑ **Transcripts (2 copies—sent to graduate school)**

❑ **Recommendations (3—sent to department)**

❑ **Writing samples (1—sent to department)**

❑ **Statement of Purpose (2 copies—sent to graduate school)**

❑ **Application form (sent to graduate school)**

❑ **Application fee—$50 (sent to graduate school)**

❑ **Acknowledgment card (sent to graduate school)**

TIP ON RECS

Collect all recommendation
letters yourself. Do not let
your recommenders send the
letters directly to the schools.
Who knows when they will get
there or if they will get there
at all?

you send it, you know it's all there. Have all official transcripts sent to you at your home address or pick them up from the school. Among the schools that I applied to, those that requested transcripts be sent directly to the school accepted transcripts sent by me, as long as they were official copies with a university seal over the flap of the envelope.

SEPTEMBER

While you're continuing to study for the GRE, you should also begin asking faculty and/or employers for recommendation letters.

What to provide to your recommenders. If you haven't already made up a curriculum vitae (CV), the academic form of a résumé, you need to do so now, particularly if you're already a master's student and plan to go on to a doctoral program. Like résumés, CVs come in a variety of formats. The sample CV here will give you an idea of what one looks like, and you can request copies of faculty CVs from your undergraduate department to see the range of formats and information included. Faculty CVs are rarely confidential—usually the department keeps several on file. If you do not have enough credentials to make a CV worthwhile, enclose a résumé.

In addition to the CV and the recommendation form itself, provide your recommenders with the following:

- *List of schools* to which you're applying, including the names of faculty you would like to work with at each school.
- *Self-addressed stamped envelopes* (addressed to your home, NOT to the graduate school or department to which you're applying). If you live close to your recommenders, do not stamp the envelopes. Instead, let your recommenders know you will come by to collect the letters yourself. Make sure they understand that they must sign the back flap of the envelopes after they have sealed them, whether you will be picking up the letters or receiving them in the mail.
- *Deadline for completing recommendation letters.* Do not ask your recommenders to keep track of several deadlines (each school you're applying to

CURRICULUM VITAE

Rachel L. Kirkland
Department of English
CB# 3520, Greenlaw Hall
University of North Carolina at Chapel Hill
Chapel Hill, NC 27599-3520
engrlk@mail.unc.edu
WWW Home Page: http://www.unc.edu/~engrlk/home.html

Fields of Interest:

Major Area: American Renaissance
Minor Area: Eighteenth-Century British Literature
Textual Editing and Criticism (print and electronic)

Education:

University of North Carolina at Chapel Hill
Ph.D. candidate in English, 4.0/4.0 GPA
Dissertation Title: "A Human Life: Being the Autobiography of Elizabeth Oakes Smith": A Critical Edition and Introduction
Dissertation Director: Dr. James Merrifield, Department Chair

Emory University
B.A. in English and Philosophy, 1990
3.8/4.0 cumulative GPA

Academic Positions and Honors:

- Pass with Distinction, doctoral examinations in American Renaissance, American Realism and Naturalism, Eighteenth-Century British Literature, Spring 1995
- Awarded $2,500 Dissertation Grant from UNC Research Office
- Member, Alpha Epsilon Lambda (national graduate student honor society)
- Southeastern Regional Director, MLA Graduate Student Caucus, 1994-95
- Editor, *Graduate Student Caucus Newsletter*, 1995

Academic Employment:

- Assistant Editor, *Eighteenth-Century Studies*, 1993-present
- Graduate Teaching Assistant, 1995-present
- Short Story, Freshman Composition, and Business Writing. Responsible for planning, teaching, and grading all sections.

Publications:

- "Property Rights of Women in the Early Eighteenth-Century: The Case of *Roxana.*" *Eighteenth-Century Fiction* 7:3 (April 1995).
- "Narrative Compression and Collapse in Elizabeth Stoddard's *The Morgesons.*" *The Journal of Narrative Technique* 26:1 (forthcoming Winter 1996)
- "Graduate Students Working for Scholarly Journals." Solicited and under review by *The Chronicle of Higher Education.*

Conferences and Presentations:

- "Comparisons of Feminine (Anti-) Virtue in Haywood's *Anti-Pamela and Defoe's* Roxana."
  Aphra Behn Society Conference (Huntington Library, 7–9 October 1994).
- "Transgressive and Transcendent Pleasures in Libertine Literature and Women's Amatory Fiction."
  Northeast American Society for Eighteenth-Century Studies (NEASECS) Conference (University of
  Ottawa, 7–10 September 1995).
- "Rituals of Damage in Elizabeth Stoddard's *The Morgesons." Modern Language Association Convention
  (Chicago, 27–30 December 1995).*

Professional Organizations:

ASECS
Association for Documentary Editing
Council of Editors of Learned Journals (CELJ)
Melville Society
MLA
MLA Graduate Student Caucus, Southeastern Regional Director
South Atlantic Modern Language Association (SAMLA)

Internet Academic Discussion Groups:

C18-L (Interdisciplinary Eighteenth-Century Discussion List)
EDITOR-L (Council of Editors of Learned Journals List)
SHARP-L (Society for the History of Authorship, Reading and Publishing List)

*For information on nonacademic publications, see résumé on World Wide Web Home Page at http://www.
unc.edu/~engrlk/home.html*

will have its own deadline). The letters will either come to you or you will pick them up, so set the deadline for a single date in November, such as November 15.

- *Research interests.* Let your recommenders know what you plan on studying in graduate school so they can comment on your potential research area.
- *Related info about yourself.* If you haven't been in class with these faculty members for awhile (or even if you have), it's a good idea to remind them of which classes you took, the dates of the classes, and your final grades. These details help to refresh their memory and comment more accurately. If you're also applying for a fellowship or assistantship, let your recommenders know so they can also recommend that you receive assistance.

OCTOBER

Good luck on your GRE! In addition to taking your test, this is the month to prepare any samples of your work that need to be included with your application, and also the time to begin ordering your transcripts.

Polishing your samples. If you're sending a writing sample, look over your college papers and pick either your strongest paper or one (or more) that matches up most closely with your prospective topic for research at each school. Then revise the paper, looking for grammar problems, false or weak logic in your argument, and careless errors in citation and formatting. Make sure your name is on the first page and included in the page numbering (ex. Mitchell 2, Mitchell 3, and so on).

Polish your style as much as you can in the paper and whittle it down or expand it to meet the page requirements for each school. If you're submitting a portfolio, you will want to rearrange it to the best advantage, according to the specialties of each school, and update it to include any of your recent work.

Have your samples proofed. You may want to ask a faculty member, the graduate director if possible, to read over your paper(s) or look over your portfolio before you send it off. If you don't or can't ask a faculty

NAME-DROPPING

If you think the admissions committee might be familiar with the professor teaching the class for which you wrote the paper, include the professor's name on the first page, along with the title and course number of the class and the date the paper was turned in.

member to check your samples, have another diligent student review it or go to your school's Writing Center and have an English tutor go over it with you. Above all, don't spend too much time on the paper(s)—they could be improved indefinitely, of course, but the admissions committee wants to see a writing sample that accurately reflects your writing and analytical skills under a typical classroom deadline.

Get your transcripts. Write or visit schools to request your official transcripts. Again, as I said before, do not send your transcripts directly to the graduate schools or departments to which you are applying. It's best to collect all of the transcripts yourself, so that you can sort them out to send to each school. And request an extra official transcript for yourself to look over. Review this transcript to make sure there are no errors in your grades, the date you received your degree, or any other problems that might reflect negatively on your admissions. If you notice anything amiss, have it corrected immediately so you can get a new set of transcripts. This is another benefit of sending transcripts yourself.

NOVEMBER

This is a big month in terms of proving yourself to the admissions committee. You will begin working on your statement of purpose (which is the term for the grad school admissions essay) and setting up campus visits to meet prospective advisers and students in the program (if the department does not arrange the interview).

Collect your recommendation letters. Don't forget that this is the month to collect your recommendation letters. Once you've received all of them, make time to write thank-you notes to all of the people that gave you a recommendation. Don't write a form letter—make each "thank you" individual and personal. Recommendations are difficult to write and time-consuming for faculty and employers, so be appreciative of their time. They may be the reason, in the end, that you get into the school of your choice.

Write a statement of purpose. Don't put this off until the last minute. While the application essay may seem like a trivial part of the application, it is the only part of the application that allows the faculty to get to know you personally. The statement of purpose is your opportunity to dazzle the admissions committee with your intelligence, maturity, focus, and compatibility with the faculty's research interests. All of the admissions officers, deans, and faculty I interviewed took this part of the application seriously, and some weighed it as the number one criterion for evaluation. In addition, many faculty regard the essay as an example of your writing skills, an important part of your graduate career whether you're pursuing English or engineering. For more information on writing your statement of purpose see Richard Stelzer's *How to Write a Winning Personal Statement*.

Focus, focus, focus! Many undergraduates consider the statement of purpose to be some kind of test of character, and begin their essays something like, "I have always loved anthropology/chemistry/history/math and want to make the world a better place by pursuing a graduate degree. . ." Don't write anything even remotely similar; it's the death blow to the essay. The selections committee is not interested in your love of the field or your moral inclinations for taking on graduate work. They want to know if you have what it takes to finish the program. More specifically, they want to know if your research interests match the department's ongoing research. Passion about the field is a given; no one decides to go to graduate school with a lukewarm interest in the discipline. You don't have to prove that you'll love what you do—you have to prove that you'll be good at what you do.

The best way to demonstrate your aptitude to the committee is to focus the essay on your intended topic of study. Present a problem that you would like to solve, or a problem that has presumably been solved but not to your satisfaction. Show the committee, in a couple of paragraphs, what research area interests you most and how you would approach studying it. If possible, say how this research would contribute to the field, i.e., stimulate a rethinking of the problem, open up new areas of investigation, or be useful in the classroom.

Explain gaps in your application. I didn't use this strategy, preferring to concentrate on my strengths, but

For the GRE General, I focused all of my energy on the verbal section; the others, I'm told, are mostly ignored in literature programs. I don't know how you can significantly improve your reading comprehension, apart from learning how to beat the test.

My energy was best spent on stuffing my head full of vocabulary— obnubiate is to anserine as mulct is to tergiversation. A handy book: I Always Look Up the Word Egregious, by Maxwell Nurnberg.

—Sean, Ph.D. student, English

EXPLAINING SPECIAL CIRCUMSTANCES

The essay is the only space you have to inform the committee about any circumstances that should be weighed with the rest of the application. When looking over your credentials with an objective eye, you may find elements that need explaining. If you decide to use this approach, my recommendation is to keep it short and sweet—no more than a sentence or two about any weaknesses in your application. Don't dwell on this part of the essay, even though your first draft will undoubtedly be lengthy with explication (and excuses!).

many students also use the application essay to smooth over weak spots in other areas of their application. If you took six years to graduate, rather than four, you may want to explain why. More importantly, if your undergraduate major is different from your intended major at the graduate level, you will want to say what motivated you to switch departments. Some students use the essay to explain low grades in certain classes or why they have submitted nonacademic recommendations rather than recs from faculty. International students may want to discuss their reasons for attending school in another country.

Hard sell. The essay is also the time to blow your own horn. Yes, we can learn from Madonna—the art of self-promotion! Some students begin their essays with a discussion of their background and academic experience first, then go on to discuss their plans for graduate study. Others start out with their proposed topic of study and then demonstrate how their experience would contribute to their projected research. I prefer the second method, although there are benefits to both. If you begin by stating your accomplishments, then a committee's first impression is that you're qualified for graduate work. If your research proposal doesn't exactly match the department's interests, the faculty may be less inclined to dismiss your application. On the other hand, if your proposed topic comes first and catches their interest, your academic or work-related experience adds credibility and offers solid evidence for pursuing the topic. Also, this second approach more closely simulates academic writing in general, in which the problem is stated first.

Whichever way you choose to structure your essay, be sure to add in any relevant experience, either academic or work-related, that contributes to your aptitude for graduate study in your field. Mention awards, honors, membership in academic or related organizations, any writing or publishing experience, and internships or work experiences that contribute to your professional maturity.

Why you're interested in the program. Finally, the statement of purpose should explain why you've chosen to apply to a particular school. Here's where all of your library grunt work—looking up programs, faculty research, facilities, and so on—pays off. If you've visited the campus, include the names of those you spoke with about the program. Mention that you've reviewed publications by Professors X, X, and X and believe your research interests are compatible with the ongoing research of these faculty members. If they have facilities that match your proposed topic of study, let them know that these special facilities stimulated your interest in applying. Many of the applicants will not have gone to the trouble to read faculty publications, and most will not even be aware of any special facilities for research.

Some students' essays discuss, at length, their interest in working with particular faculty or comment extensively on the work being done by faculty members. It's up to you how much space you use to explain your reasons for applying. Make sure, however, that no matter how much time you spend, you also include information about yourself that demonstrates your aptitude for graduate study.

Interviews. Some of you will be scheduled for campus interviews by the department. If so, you can still benefit from the tips included for students who handle campus visits on their own.

Call and let the secretary of the graduate studies office know that you are interested in visiting the campus and meeting with faculty and grad students. A diligent and committed department will have campus visit procedures already in place for prospective students, including the opportunity for you to stay with a graduate student during your visit, saving you money on a hotel. Take a look at Chapter 4, "Orientation: Once You're In," to get an idea of the kinds of questions you might want to ask faculty and grad students about the program, including scheduling a campus tour in advance. Make sure that you have gotten in touch with faculty and students beforehand to schedule times to meet (don't just drop in!), and remind them a couple of days before you arrive of any appointments you've scheduled.

Dress code. I took the advice that I should dress a little more formally than the students for my campus visit, and I was sorry I did. When I visited my first campus I chose a casual but nice denim dress that wouldn't bat an eyelash at my own school. But there I

"A GRAD STUDENT WALKS INTO A BAR . . ."

Some students take the risk of adding humor or entertaining anecdotes in their essays to stand out among the other applicants. I would say that, if humor is your style and you're comfortable with it, fire away! But if you're unsure at all about your ability to elicit yuks from the crowd, stick with the sober and focused approach.

Humor is undoubtedly a welcome relief to faculty members reading hundreds of essays, but keep in mind that what's funny to one professor may be offensive to another. Dry wit seems to be the most common and appreciated form of humor in the academy, even to the point of cynicism, but this brand of humor is not appropriate for your application.

There's a (jaded) joke floating around about grad student poverty, "You may be a graduate student if you wonder how long you can eat pasta without getting scurvy . . . " but it would be unwise to incorporate this kind of witticism in your essay!

USE YOUR UNDERGRAD RESEARCH

If you have an undergraduate paper that motivated your interest in the proposed topic of study, be sure to mention it. This shows the committee that you have researched the problem before and demonstrates your interest in research from your undergraduate days. The committee wants to see how you became interested in your research objectives, including your aptitude for conducting research.

UNRELATED EXPERIENCE

Sometimes even indirectly related skills can be an advantage. One student I know had a background in art. When she applied to graduate school in English, she presented her undergraduate art degree as an interdisciplinary strength that separated her from other candidates with a background solely in English. Her strategy worked—she was accepted to several top English programs. If you have unrelated experiences you think would make you stand out from the other applicants, highlight them in the essay.

got stared at like an invading alien all over campus—every student I passed was dressed super casually in jeans, sweater, coat, and gloves. I stood out like a sore thumb and felt awkward all day long. By the time I made my next campus visit I had learned my lesson and had dressed down to casual pants and a sweater, still a tad more formal than the general student attire. I felt very comfortable and the students and faculty seemed comfortable with me. For what it's worth, I would say that you should try to fit in with the grad students as much as possible during the campus visit—try to look like one of them.

DECEMBER

Yes, it's almost over—you're ready to send everything in the mail. When you send the application, be sure to make copies of everything you're sending, including a copy of your check for the application fee and copies of the sealed envelopes containing recommendations and transcripts. The copies won't help you too much if your application gets lost in the mail—you'll need to reorder transcripts and get more recs—but at least you'll know exactly what you sent to each school, and you will have a copy of the application form itself.

CALLING ABOUT YOUR APPLICATION STATUS

If you sent everything yourself, you just have to wait for your acknowledgment card to arrive. You know that if they received your application then they have all of the application materials. If you had to send transcripts, recs, or other items separate from the application, be prepared to spend hours on the phone verifying with the schools that all of your materials have arrived. The phones will be jammed with similar calls—another reason I recommend sending all of your application materials yourself.

Once your application is complete, all you have to do is wait. Don't be surprised if it's April and you still don't have an answer. Some departments may not let you know if you're accepted until May, but it's much more common for schools to give you a decision by the end of March.

FINANCIAL AID

The only aid I got was my assistantship and I would encourage everyone to get one if possible. Not only did it pay well but it gave me valuable experience, which was a key factor in getting the job I now have.

—Erik, M.A. graduate, Education

Recent statistics from the U.S. Department of Education report that 60 percent of doctoral students and 40 percent of master's students receive financial aid. Both inside and outside the academy, the traditional view is that graduate school constitutes a full-time job, and students should be funded well enough that they do not need to seek outside employment to finish a degree. Universities have an incentive to offer aid to students in the form of assistantships, which provide cheap labor for teaching core curriculum classes and conducting research.

Don't expect to live like a king. The majority of financial aid is provided by the university, with federal aid a secondary source of support. The most common forms of aid, fellowship and assistantship awards, can be as high as $17,000 per year; this is in addition to a waiver on tuition and fees. Unfortunately, this may be the only financial support you receive, unless you take out a loan. While a university award may provide enough money to live on, it ensures a relatively spartan existence. Attending conferences paid for by the university replaces going on regular vacations, and the low living allowance keeps you from getting distracted from your studies. After all, the library is free!

APPLYING FOR AID

Most financial aid can be applied for through your university. By requesting to be considered for aid on your admissions application, you will automatically be considered for assistantships, university fellowships, and outside fellowships administered by the university. For federal aid such as loans, you will need to apply through the Financial Aid Office. A quick glance at the university catalog will verify the steps you need to take to apply for aid. Even though you may not be eligible to receive need-based aid, most of the fellowships awarded by universities are based on academic merit or special status, such as being a member of a minority group or being a woman studying in a particular field. Even Federal Stafford Loans, which in the past have been based on need, can now be obtained for students who do not demonstrate financial need, provided they are willing to make the interest payments while still in school.

M.A./M.S. vs. Ph.D. awards. Before defining the types of aid available, a few caveats are in order. Master's students do not typically receive the generous funding that doctoral students receive, and if you're weighing the decision to pursue a master's versus a Ph.D., this should be an important factor to consider. On average, doctoral students receive $11,786 per year in aid, excluding loans, compared to $4,211 for master's students. Many schools don't even offer aid packages to first-year master's students; they are waiting to see if these students have the ability and determination to succeed in the program. If you're planning to continue on to the doctoral level anyway, you will probably want to go ahead and apply for a doctoral program that allows the option of a terminal master's degree along the way. Also, doctoral students in the sciences and in engineering receive significantly more financial aid than students in the humanities.

In addition, the aid awarded by the university in the first year may not be the maximum amount of aid you can receive. Once you're in school you can usually establish residency, which significantly reduces your tuition amount, and you can make contacts within the department that lead to teaching or research assistantship offers.

ASSISTANTSHIPS

Assistantships are the most common form of aid to graduate students. They require service from the student in exchange for a tuition waiver and living stipend that ranges from $5,000 to $14,000 per year. While the amount covering tuition is usually not considered taxable income, you do have to pay income taxes on the stipend.

Teaching vs. research assistantships. Assistantships are categorized as either research assistantships or teaching assistantships. Typically, the department selects the candidates who receive this type of aid, and you will be considered automatically when you apply to graduate school. Most application forms have a box that you check if you wish to be considered for this type of aid. Some schools include an additional application form for assistantships; others wait until you have been accepted before sending you a separate application form, which requests more specific information about your credentials for research or your teaching background. In rare cases, the assistantships are more competitive, and the university graduate school will select candidates. In such cases it is common for the graduate school to base its recommendations on standardized criteria such as GPA or GRE test scores. They may also require an essay from you explaining why you need the money and ask you to describe your intended area of specialization.

Research assistantships (RAs). These are more commonly offered to students in the biological, physical, and social sciences than are teaching assistantships. If you receive a research assistantship in the sciences you will be required to contribute 20 hours per week in the laboratory, generally working under the supervision of a faculty adviser. Your laboratory work is part of the adviser's own research project, and the funds may come from outside grants supporting the project or from the university. Be aware, however, that because you are working for a specific project/supervisor, the "required"

RA OR TA?

In many cases, your dissertation will come directly out of your work as a research assistant. For this reason, an RA position may be a more advantageous award than a TA in the sciences because the lab work is a shortcut in the dissertation process.

THE REWARDS OF TEACHING

Most grad students receiving TAs view teaching as a welcome change from the monotony of research for their thesis or dissertation. Students granted a teaching assistantship will work with a number of professors during the tenure of the award, which has proven to be a good way to get to know prospective advisers and get recognition from other faculty in the department.

You may find that after the isolating experience of conducting library research and pursuing a single topic for a number of years, teaching offers much-needed perspective and helps anchor you within the university community.

Also, for TAs in the sciences who have to pass qualifying exams based on coursework, keeping their feet wet in the basics helps them to be better prepared.

And finally, job opportunities within the academic community require a Ph.D. plus teaching credentials, so a TA position could help you decide early in your program if an academic career is right for you.

hours are fluid, and you may be working during the summer whether or not you are paid for the hours. Extra work will sometimes be "paid" by a professor in the form of coauthorship of a publication. If you've carried out a substantial portion of the research for the submitted article, your name will be credited along with your supervising professor.

Humanities RAs. Research assistantships in the humanities are similar to those in the sciences in that your research is supervised by a faculty member. You may spend time in the library working on his or her book project, checking citations, updating research, or collating bibliographies. In many cases you will be doing the grunt work too—making copies, printing and mailing chapters, or entering the faculty adviser's handwritten revisions into the computer. As in the sciences, the professor may have an outside grant for the assistantship funds, such as a National Endowment for the Humanities grant, or he or she may be financially supported by the university.

Teaching assistantships (TAs). If you're an incoming grad student in the sciences, teaching assistantships may be offered to you until you find a research project or lab to join and receive an RA appointment. A TA in the sciences will not generally serve as an instructor, but will be asked by the instructor to help grade papers, supervise laboratories, or lead classroom discussion groups for intro science classes. In some cases, you will be allowed to teach courses, either intro or upper-division, and may have the freedom to choose the textbook and create the syllabus for the course. TAs who assist an instructor are typically required to work 20 hours per week.

Teaching assistantships in the humanities are offered to students who have completed at least some part of their course work. TAs teach an intro course in their field, such as Freshman Composition, although in some cases a TA may be allowed to design and teach an upper-division course. If a TA is offered to you while you are still finishing course work, keep in mind that the university expects you to maintain a full-time schedule while teaching. Also, depending on the school, some TAs will not be expected to teach, but only to assist the instructor. In general, however, a TA in the humanities will be in charge of the classroom.

For students required to teach intro courses in their field, most departments provide orientation seminars to help them become acquainted with the rudiments of teaching the course, including university-wide requirements on textbooks and syllabi. Depending on the university, an orientation seminar may last a few hours or may be an intensive six-week prep course. For more information on teaching, see Chapter 6.

GRANTS

Grants are funds awarded that do not have to be paid back, including fellowships and scholarships or tuition waivers. You may have the impression that grants are research funding available only to advanced doctoral or postdoctoral students. Not true. There are directories of grant sources that frequently list fellowships and other forms of aid for beginning students. For example, Oryx Press publishes the *Directory of Research Grants* in three volumes, divided by field (humanities, physical sciences, and biomedical and health care), and the subject index lists both "Fellowships" and "Student Support." Other selected grant sources are listed in Chapter 7 and in the annotated bibliography at the back of this book.

Research grants may be awarded to individuals carrying out dissertation research, but more commonly, grants are awarded to universities. Large research grants provided by the government or outside agencies award money to universities to carry out specific projects. The university passes on the research funds to the department, and the faculty members, in turn, pay students out of these funds for research assistantships. A faculty member may have an idea for a particular research project, and he or she will contact the research office at the university to find out which granting institution is most likely to fund such a project. In some cases, a professor will already have an idea of the best agency to apply to, and the research office handles only the administrative components of the application. The largest funding for grants to universities comes from the

"I'D LIKE TO THANK THE ACADEMY. . . "

The experience of regular public speaking, which comes with teaching, can help you conquer whatever stage fright you've carried over from your undergrad days and provide the skills you will need later in defending your thesis or passing an oral exam before a faculty panel.

GRANTS MEAN BIG BUCKS

Grants are the largest source of research funding for universities, and knowing how the grant process operates can help you even in the early phases of your graduate career. This is especially true in the sciences. In fact, grant-writing is such a significant part of a career in the physical sciences that many students are required to draft a sample grant proposal and defend it as part of their oral exams.

National Science Foundation (NSF), the National Endowment for the Humanities (NEH), and the National Institutes of Health (NIH).

Grants to individuals. Grants to individuals conducting research are less common, but funding is available for them. Like grant funding for institutions, individual research grants are specialized according to the needs of the institution granting the money. You will be carrying out their research and then using the information for your own dissertation. For this reason, even with the staggering number of grants available through private sources and the government, it can still be difficult to locate funding that matches your own interests. If you haven't decided on a research project for your dissertation, you may want to consult the listings of grants in your field and look for ongoing projects that might be of interest to you as a dissertation topic. For more information on preparing grant proposals, see Chapter 7.

FELLOWSHIPS

For incoming graduate students, receipt of a fellowship represents the highest level of prestige and academic freedom, and the generous monetary awards for fellowships reflect this elite status. Fellowships are not generally offered to master's students, but usually only to highly qualified Ph.D. candidates. Fellowships are "free" money, covering the cost of tuition and fees and offering a stipend without requiring service from the student. Once in grad school, the benefits of having a fellowship are enormous. You may be approached by various faculty members who want you to be part of their research teams or individual projects. A fellowship means that you do not have the financial need to jump immediately into an adviser's research project and can spend time selecting an adviser or a research project suited to your interests. It also means that you have more time to decide on a thesis or dissertation topic, without the service constraints of an assistantship. One factor to consider, however, is that without an RA position, your research will be primarily self-directed, and having to learn the ropes on your own may slow your progress. Weigh the advantages of both types of awards, particularly if you are going into the sciences.

TYPES OF FELLOWSHIPS

The most common types of fellowships are granted by the university graduate school and they are *extremely* competitive. A university may only offer ten awards to be distributed among all of the entering graduate students. Because the competition is intense, you may be required to apply for these fellowships in advance of the deadline for application to graduate school. In addition to the standardized criteria used by the graduate school, such as GPA (usually minimum 3.5 overall) and GRE scores (combined verbal/quantitative 1400), you will also be evaluated by your prospective department. The graduate school may make their selection based on the recommendation of the department or by a faculty member who will serve as your adviser. Outside of the university, the following fellowship programs, listed by field of study, are among the largest awards granted to beginning students.

Biology *Hughes Predoctoral Fellowships.* These fellowships are offered to graduate students who have completed less than a year of full-time study. The application is open to U.S. and international students, and the deadline is November 5. Call 202-334-2872 for an application and more information. In 1993, 1,500 applications were received and 80 fellowships were awarded.

Arts, Humanities, and Social Sciences *Jacob K. Javits Graduate Fellowships.* These fellowships are open to doctoral students who have not yet completed more than 20 semester hours of study. Application deadline is February 1, and you can call 202-260-3574 for an application and more information. In 1993, 2,750 applications were received and 89 fellowships were awarded. In 1994, 5,500 applications were received and 86 fellowships were awarded.

Humanities *Mellon Fellowships.* These are for graduate students who will ultimately pursue teaching. The

OUTSIDE FUNDING

Funding for university awards is usually supplemented by outside sources. These sources include private endowments, corporate contributions to facilitate research, foundation contributions, and government agencies.

In some cases, these agencies may offer independent fellowships, meaning the award goes directly to you rather than through the university, and you can use the award at the school of your choice.

DISSERTATION/TRAVEL FELLOWSHIPS

Research universities often provide awards to advanced graduate students working on their dissertations or presenting papers/posters at conferences.

Dissertation fellowships help fund unusual expenses associated with completing a dissertation, including travel to specialized libraries or research institutions, equipment and materials, and payment of lab subjects or consultants.

Travel fellowships pay for a student to participate in conferences for which a student's research paper has been accepted for presentation.

awards are for one year only, although students making satisfactory progress may be eligible for money during dissertation writing. Both U.S. and Canadian citizens are eligible, and students cannot have completed any graduate study at the time of application. You must be nominated by the Mellon coordinator on your campus, and the deadline for nomination is November 1. The completed application is due November 30. Call 609-924-4713 for details. In 1993, 1,043 applications were received and 101 fellowships were awarded.

Science and Engineering *National Science Foundation Graduate Research Fellowships.* Awards are open to master's and doctoral students who have not completed more than 20 semester hours or 30 quarter hours of graduate study. The program is open to U.S. citizens only, and the deadlines are November 5 for Part I and December 3 for Part II. Contact the NSF at Oak Ridge Institute for Science and Education, P. O. Box 3010, Oak Ridge, TN, 37831-3010 or call 423-241-4300 for an application and more information. In 1993, 6,222 applications were received and 950 fellowships were awarded.

National Defense Science and Engineering Graduate Fellowship Program. Offered by the U.S. Department of Defense, this program is open to graduate students who are near the beginning of graduate study, and the award continues for three years. The program is offered for U.S. citizens only, and you can receive more information and an application by contacting Dr. George Outterson at 919-549-8505.

Office of Naval Research Graduate Fellowship Program. For beginning graduate students who are U.S. citizens. Award is renewable for three years. The deadline is January 15, and you can receive an application and more information by calling 202-331-3500. In 1993, approximately 1,000 applications were received and 40 fellowships were awarded.

OTHER SOURCES OF AID

Residence Hall Director. This is a source of aid often overlooked by prospective graduate students. If you're a single student coming to a new city without a network of friends, a residence hall position will not only help with your expenses, it will also help to orient you within the university community. Like TA and RA positions, the award is based on service. You will supervise undergraduate students in residence halls, and the award offers, at the very minimum, room and board. Some awards also carry a stipend. University requirements differ on their criteria for selection. Some schools wish to interview the applicant beforehand, while others require the student to have lived in residence for a period of time before being considered. Married students are not eligible for this type of aid.

Work-Study Program. Federal work-study assistance is not limited to undergraduate students, but some departments frown on this type of aid at the graduate level if the work does not directly contribute to your program of study. Most universities require that you gain permission from the graduate office before taking a work-study job. Work-study opportunities are similar for undergrads and grad students, offering jobs on campus. In some cases, you can obtain an administrative position within your department as a work-study student.

Because work-study is a federally funded program, you will be required to submit a completed application for federal student aid through the financial aid office. Eligibility for the work-study program is based on financial need. Some requirements for this type of aid include good standing on undergraduate federal education loans (Staffords, Perkins, etc.), U.S. citizenship or eligible alien status, and registration for Selective Service if applicable. A listing of job opportunities available on campus is provided by the financial aid office, but it would also be a good idea to contact the department you're applying to and find out if it offers administrative assistantships or work-study opportunities within the department.

Scholarships or tuition waivers. Based on the recommendation of the department to which you are applying, the graduate school may grant tuition waivers. Primarily targeted to out-of-state residents to encourage enrollment, this award may take the form of a total tuition waiver or a reduced tuition equal to in-state fees. Some universities also offer tuition scholarships to both in-state and out-of-state students that cover the full cost

WORK-STUDY AS RA

Another creative use of the work-study program is to work for a professor conducting lab research. If you are not awarded an RA but wish to work under the supervision of a particular faculty member, it's a good idea to contact the professor and propose that you be a work-study student in his or her lab.

Since the federal government pays 75 percent of your wage, a professor can support you under a research grant for a fraction of the cost of an additional RA appointment.

PAYING TAXES

International students, like U.S. citizens, are taxed on money awarded as a TA or RA stipend and you should consult the Internal Revenue Service (IRS) on the procedures for paying taxes. The Institute for International Education publishes a number of helpful guides for international students, including *Funding for U.S. Study: A Guide for Foreign Nationals*, which you can obtain by contacting the IIE at 809 United Nations Plaza, New York, NY, 10017-3580, USA.

of tuition and fees. Be sure to confirm with the university the requirements for this type of award. In many cases, the course catalog does not specify that the tuition waiver is in exchange for service, such as a TA or RA assignment.

Internships/traineeships/co-ops. Requirements vary for these programs, but in most cases the university participates with an outside company for internships and co-op programs. These companies employ you in exchange for a salary. You may work part-time or full-time, and, in the case of co-op programs, you may take quarters/semesters off from school to work full-time. You may also be eligible to receive course credit for your employment in addition to wages. These educational opportunities are generally offered to students in the sciences who conduct research overseen by their faculty advisers and job supervisors; however, these kinds of employment are expanding to include humanities and business-related degree programs.

Traineeships are less common and pay a stipend that does not require you to perform a service as long as you are making satisfactory progress toward a Ph.D. The department applies for these traineeships through federal or other agencies, and the faculty determines which students will receive the awards. If the traineeship is through an outside research organization you may be paid to work for the organization during the summer.

INTERNATIONAL STUDENTS

The unwelcome news for international students is that, according to the Council of Graduate Schools, about half of all enrolled international students support themselves through their own private resources. Most students who do receive aid are funded by the university in the form of RAs and TAs, and the largest nonservice awards are given to international students in the fields of natural sciences and engineering. Some universities have an international student aid adviser on campus who can give you detailed information about financial aid offered by the university and answer questions about restrictions for employment. Below is a list of some of the most common funding sources available to international graduate students.

TERI loans. These loans are provided by The Education Resources Institute, and eligibility is determined by the credit worthiness of the borrower. You can have a co-borrower who is a U.S. citizen apply for the loan if you are not a citizen yourself. Loan amounts vary and the loan is not based on financial need. Contact TERI at 1-800-225-TERI for more information and an application.

GradSHARE and GradEXCEL. International students may be eligible for loans through the GradSHARE or GradEXCEL loan programs offered by Nellie Mae. You can borrow up to the maximum cost of your education with a creditworthy co-borrower under GradEXCEL. To be eligible for GradSHARE, you have to be attending one of the thirty-two-member schools that make up the Consortium on Financing Higher Education. Under the GradEXCEL program, you can attend any accredited, degree-granting college or university in the United States. Contact your prospective university or Nellie Mae directly at 1-800-634-9308 for more information about eligibility.

Hughes Predoctoral Fellowships in the Biological Sciences. See description above under "Fellowships."

Mellon Fellowships in the Humanities. Open to Canadian students. See description above under "Fellowships."

MINORITIES AND WOMEN

Because universities are trying to recruit more minority students for graduate education, several generous sources of funding are available for minority students on the basis of ethnic background alone. Typically, fellowships are available not only through the Graduate School but also through a number of outside sources, including the U.S. Department of Education. Most waive tuition and fees and offer a yearly stipend ranging from $2,000 to $14,000 for beginning students. Application for these fellowships is usually made through the graduate school, and these awards may be need- or merit-based. Below are some of the biggest awards offered to minority and women students.

Ford Foundation Doctoral Fellowships for Minorities. This three-year fellowship is open to minority

FUNDING FOR WOMEN

Women students have an advantage studying in the sciences or engineering in terms of financial aid over women studying in other disciplines. Because women, like minorities, have been "traditionally underrepresented" in these fields, several government grant programs, along with the university itself, target funding to women students.

The Educational Testing Service (ETS) makes the process of fitting a minority student with a prospective program easier through the GRE application. If you check the box on the GRE form for the "Graduate Student Locator Service," you will be contacted by schools that are trying to increase their minority enrollment.

The form asks questions regarding racial or ethnic background; intended field of specialization; degree objective; state of residence; and geographic preference of university.

The ETS also offers a helpful publication, *Graduate and Professional School Opportunities for Minority Students,* which you can obtain for free by calling the ETS at 609-771-7243.

students in all fields of study. Ford offers predoctoral fellowships, dissertation fellowships, and postdoctoral fellowships. The application is due in early November, and you can call 202-334-2872 to request the application and more information. In 1993, 1,100 applications for the predoctoral fellowship were received, and 55 fellowships were awarded.

National Science Foundation Minority Graduate Fellowships. Open to minority students who have completed 30 or fewer semester hours of graduate study. In 1993, 1,086 applications were received and 150 fellowships were awarded. See description above under "Fellowships: National Science Foundation Graduate Research Fellowships."

Patricia Roberts Harris Fellowship. These fellowships are awarded to both master's and doctoral minority and women students, generally in mathematics and the sciences where these candidates have been traditionally underrepresented. The award provides a stipend for up to four years of study, and contributes to tuition and fees. These awards are administered by the university, and you can contact the university for information, deadlines, and an application.

Other sources. The Bureau of Indian Affairs offers financial aid to students who are at least one-quarter American Indian or Alaskan native and are from a federally recognized tribe. For more information, call 202-208-3711. For women going to graduate school in the sciences, you can order *Grants-at-a-Glance* by calling 202-326-8940, which emphasizes science fellowship opportunities for women.

LOANS

With so many other sources of aid available to graduate students, loans should be your last recourse. If you have already accumulated debt from your undergraduate institutions, the prospects of graduating with an advanced degree, job hunting in a crowded field, and the hypersensitivity of potential employers to your credit rating will only be exacerbated by the baggage of extra educational debt. Particularly for married students or students with families, the lack of income combined with accumulating debt may act as obstacles to concentrating on academic work and keeping things going smoothly at home.

Ask yourself seriously if you want to make this kind of financial commitment before you decide "It's Harvard or bust!" In the 1980s, many undergraduate students took out loans, banking that a better school would yield a better job, but many college grads have found that a degree from a good school is no insulation against a difficult entry-level job market.

Having said that, Congressional statistics reflect that two-thirds of all graduate students use loans to supplement their financial aid resources. For public school students, the yearly average debt accumulated is $8,000; for private university students, the average is $12,000. Federal loans allow students to borrow up to $18,500 per year, and thus can substitute for the absence of a stipend. When doing preliminary estimates on the amount you need to borrow, keep in mind the possibility that your dissertation research may take longer than the grad school catalog claims, and if your other funding runs out, you'll be relying on loans to complete your degree.

The most common loan programs are the Stafford Student Loans, Perkins Loans, and the new Federal Direct Student Loan. Beginning in July 1994, the Supplemental Loans for Students (SLS) program merged into the Federal Direct Student Loan program, explained later in the chapter. See the table on page 56 for the requirements of Stafford and Perkins Loans.

Students should not wait for acceptance to a program of study before applying for loans. The standardized form for federal loans is called the FAFSA (Free Application for Federal Student Assistance), although schools may use different forms depending on their individual needs, including the more detailed GAPSFAS, FAF, CSS, or ACT forms. Some of these forms require a processing fee from the student. The FAFSA can be filled out after January 1 before the school year for which you are applying for aid. For example, if you want aid for the 1997–98 school year, complete the FAFSA after January 1, 1997. This form can also be used to apply for state-awarded aid, and on it you will find a list of state application deadlines. In many

MAKING A DECISION

Many graduate students claim that the primary factor in deciding between universities was the amount of aid they were offered by each. A "name" school acceptance with no aid award took second place for many students to a less prestigious university that offered a full fellowship.

WHY DO STUDENTS DROP OUT?

The Council of Graduate Schools reports that the most common cause of not finishing a degree program is a lack of financial support during the dissertation research process.

A HANDY BOOK

For information on the complexities of the process of determining the amount you will be allowed to borrow, your best source is *Financing Graduate School*, 2nd edition, by Patricia McWade, Dean of Financial Student Services at Georgetown University.

LOAN COMPARISON TABLE		
	Federal Stafford Loan	*Federal Perkins Loan*
Annual Loan Limit:	Current law = $8,500	$5,000
Cumulative Loan Limit:	Current law = $65,500	$30,000
Annual Interest Rate:	NA	0% in school; 5% in repayment
Variable Interest Rate:	0% in school; 91-day T Bill rate plus 2.5% while not in school	NA
Need-Based Aid:	Yes	Yes
Application Fee:	None	None
Credit Worthiness Test:	None	None
Origination Fee:	1%	None
Guarantee Fee:	0-3%	None
Form of Disbursement:	Wired or check to the school depending on the lender	Credited to student's account in two equal installments each semester
Deferments:	No repayment while in school, some deferments after graduation	No repayment while in school, some deferments after graduation
Prepayment Penalty:	No	No
Grace Period:	6 months	9 months; 6 months for old National Direct Student Loans
Minimum Monthly Payment:	$50	$40
Length of Repayment:	Up to 10 years; can consolidate	Up to 10 years; can consolidate

cases, the state deadline may come before the federal deadline, and many states request that you check with the university financial aid officer for specific state deadlines at each school you wish to attend. The deadline for receipt of the FAFSA is May 1, but you'll need to check with the school if you are required to submit a separate or additional financial aid form.

Your application for federal aid must be renewed each year, so make sure you reapply in time to be considered. Also, unlike service-related sources of aid, loans are nontaxable. For the purposes of receiving federal aid, graduate students are automatically considered independent regardless of age, although a few schools will still require income information about your parents and, based on their previous year's tax forms, may require a contribution from them toward your school expenses. To be eligible for federal loans, you must be a U.S. citizen or eligible noncitizen. Your financial aid office or library may have the Student Loan Counselor software offered by ETS. This financial aid software package asks you questions about your indebtedness and career plans, and offers guidelines for your debt management. You can also call the Federal Student Aid Information Center at 1-800-433-3243 for details about federal programs and financial aid awarded individually by state.

Federal Direct Student Loans. This is a fairly new program, beginning in the 1994–95 school year, that allows a student to receive loans directly through the U.S. Department of Education. If you received Federal Stafford Loans as an undergraduate, they were processed through a private lender, which sent checks to your financial aid office and were guaranteed against default by the government. The new Federal Direct Student Loans eliminate the middle step of the private lender; the government gives your loan funds directly to the university. Graduate students are eligible to receive both subsidized and unsubsidized direct loans through this program. Subsidized direct loans are similar to the traditional Stafford Loans, which are based on need, and the government pays the interest on your loan while you are still in school. The unsubsidized direct loans are not based on need, and interest payments will be charged to you while you are enrolled. The loan amount cannot exceed the cost of your education, as determined by the university, minus other financial aid you receive. Basically, this means that the loan amount you request on the application will be reduced by the financial aid office if you are already receiving a fellowship, assistantship, etc.

The maximum interest rate for a direct loan is 8.25 percent, making it a very attractive borrowing option, but you will also be charged an administrative fee of 4 percent of the total amount of the loan, which you should take into account when deciding on the amount you want to request. You may apply for direct loans through the financial aid office of your grad school. Like other federal loans, you are automatically considered an independent student if you will be enrolling as a graduate student.

OTHER LOAN SERVICES

Participation in the Federal Direct Student Loan program is decided individually by each university, and at present not all schools participate. Major national banks trying to compete with this new program have formed a consortium called Educational Loan Management Partners, which proposes to disburse funds electronically to schools. According to a recent article from *American Banker*, the private banks hope to process loans more quickly and cheaply, providing benefits to students comparable to the Federal Direct Student Loan program. If your school doesn't offer the Federal Direct Student Loan program, they may offer this alternative in its place.

NEGOTIATING FOR MORE $$$

Once you have received acceptance letters with various financial aid packages, you'll have to make the hardest decision: choosing among the different offers. Robert L. Peters, in his book *Getting What You Came For: The Smart Student's Guide To Earning a Master's or a Ph.D.*, suggests that you may be able to "haggle" with the department or financial aid office if you've received an unsatisfactory offer. If your first-choice school offers a low financial aid amount, but your second-choice school is offering a solid financial aid package, Peters recommends contacting the first school and finding out if they can improve their initial offer. Some schools must put their financial aid packages together before their actual funding has been received, which usually happens after July 1, the new fiscal year for universities.

In addition, some students awarded aid will decide on other universities, particularly top candidates who will receive large amounts of aid at all of the schools to which they apply, and their funds will be freed up to another worthy student (maybe you!). Also, some departments do not completely budget all of their financial resources, so there may be more money available for you if you let the department know that you'll be forced to choose another school unless you can get more financial support from them.

ORIENTATION: ONCE YOU'RE IN

We had an orientation, but the hardest questions were the ones the orientation team wouldn't think of answering, and I didn't think to ask: "Will I have a social life?" (No) "Will I end up hating my thesis?" (Yes) "Can I take a term off?" (No) "Will I get free e-mail?" (Yes).

—Patrick, M.A. student, English

In my survey, students frequently said that the official orientation program was over long before they even knew the right questions to ask! For most of us, orientation is an ongoing process, from the moment we begin thinking about grad school to the day we have a degree in hand.

The key to succeeding in all aspects of your graduate career is networking—with other grad students, with faculty, with administrators. Making contacts from the very beginning not only provides you with necessary information about your program, but it also yields potential opportunities. All roads lead to employment: heightened visibility in the department can help you get attractive financial aid offers, research leads, glowing letters of recommendation, and introductions by your faculty members to their colleagues at other universities. Don't make the undergraduate assumption that your reputation rests solely on academic credits. Without actively seeking information or assistance, you diminish your prospects and run the risk of falling

A student from out of state asked my adviser if he knew any of the grad students who would share their experiences with the program. When I heard this, I said "sure, give her my number!" We talked a couple of times on the phone, and she ended up coming out to stay with us while getting an apartment and stuff. I think more grad students should volunteer to help out like that, getting new students acquainted with the program and the area. It can be a good experience for all involved!

—Anna Maria, M.S. student, Psychology

behind more competitive peers. The suggestions outlined in this chapter offer tips on finding information and developing networking skills you'll need throughout your graduate career.

YOU'RE ON YOUR OWN

From our days as undergrads, we're used to getting constant feedback on our efforts—either in the form of grades or guidance from administrators who keep track of our course requirements for completing the degree. Because incoming grad students are accustomed to this process, they often register for classes without seeking any outside assistance. They assume that all important information about the details of their programs will somehow be provided for them as they get to each stage. This is a dangerous assumption. In reality, this information is almost never volunteered; graduate students must seek it out, actively educate themselves about what's ahead. It's important to take initiative, to learn everything you can about your university and its program up front.

DON'T WAIT—ASK QUESTIONS NOW!

Most of us only ask questions when something's gone wrong—we don't receive our paychecks, we're denied registration access, or our advisers are continually dissatisfied with our work. And by the time we recognize the problem, it's too late to fix it. I know students who had to switch dissertation topics two years into their research because they didn't ask the right questions early on. It's important to be determined and creative about getting information.

HOW DO GRAD STUDENTS GET INFORMATION?

Mostly we ask other grad students. I think of grad school as similar to starting a new job. My boss tells me the basic "here's what we need you to do," but I always go to my coworkers for crucial information, from where to find the bathroom to what kinds of behavior will tick off the boss. It's a faux pas to approach a prospective adviser with, "So, how's that research funding coming along?" But you still need the information before you select a research project and an adviser. Some grad students have been forced to change schools because their advisers lost the research funds that provided their financial support.

Talking to senior grad students can provide information you won't get from any other source: inside stuff about the politics of the department, the personalities of the faculty members, and the emphasis of both the department and the university on graduate student concerns. You can get information from other sources as well so that you have a consensus about the expectations of your school.

EXTRINSIC AND INTRINSIC INFO

As a beginning student, you need both extrinsic and intrinsic information. Extrinsic information answers basic "where" and "how" questions about the university, such as the location of the library, bookstore, and computer center and the availability of public transportation or on-campus parking. If you haven't moved yet, you might want to live close to other grad students, or need information about the area. In addition, you'll need input on getting insurance, doing paperwork for an assistantship, and registering for classes. For married students and those with families, some of the biggest concerns in changing locations are housing, child care, and spousal employment. Once you have an idea of the financial aid you've been awarded, you'll also want specifics on how and when you get paid by the university.

COURSE WORK IS ONLY PART OF YOUR DEGREE

Grad school is almost entirely self-directed. Except for your course work, which is a small portion the overall requirements for a degree, the only person who really monitors your progress is you. In fact, because of the tendency to inflate grades at the graduate level, even the feedback you get from faculty members about your course work may not be a clear indicator of how you're doing. It may tell you very little about how you're progressing in terms of eventually passing comps or completing a thesis or dissertation. Many times the course work is unrelated to your eventual research.

DEPARTMENT ORIENTATION

Sometimes the department itself handles the orientation session, and again the quality of the program is a good indicator of the overall emphasis of the department on graduate student concerns.

A common orientation event is a departmental mixer where new students can meet the faculty, staff, and other graduate students. Although these events are geared to socializing rather than to offering packaged information about your program, mixers allow you to meet other students as well as faculty members.

Some students have felt pressured to be brilliant in front of the faculty, as if they were being graded on their conversation at this first meeting.

Nonetheless, it's still a good idea to go to a departmental mixer, even if you're more of a wallflower than a social butterfly. Senior graduate students typically will seek you out and answer questions before you ask them. It wasn't so long ago that these grad students were in your shoes, and they remember what it's like to be just starting out.

Intrinsic information offers more subtle answers to questions about graduate "life." What is the department culture, and how do you fit in? After doing all the preparation to get into a program, everybody wants success, not surprises. Many new students have a tough time making the transition to grad school because they aren't given any information in the beginning about adopting new study habits and developing a less formal relationship with the faculty. The course catalog is no help here, nor can it detail the responsibilities of your TA or RA assignment or tell you how to manage your time or pick an adviser and committee. Then there's the big question: "What is grad school really like?"

UNIVERSITY ORIENTATION PROGRAMS

Understandably, university orientation programs are designed to answer only extrinsic questions. Many schools don't offer orientation programs at all, and others only offer programs on university teaching requirements for incoming TA's. An orientation program bears the unique character stamp of the university, and its effectiveness in indoctrinating new students reflects the kind of assistance you can expect from the graduate office and your department on other issues. A conscientious university will have a graduate student association on campus. These groups often offer the best orientation programs because of the students' ability to answer both extrinsic and intrinsic questions. They frequently hold informal get-togethers in which new students can ask detailed questions about graduate life.

THE DO-IT-YOURSELF ORIENTATION

Whether or not your university offers an orientation program, you can get the information you need without an agonizing trial-and-error period that can cost you time and money. The following is a "Do-It-Yourself" orientation program that can answer the FAQs (Frequently Asked Questions) about graduate school. Your individual needs for using these suggestions will vary, depending on the information you gained during the admissions process. Remember, the key to this personalized approach is to get a consensus from different sources. Don't assume that the first opinion you hear is correct. An older professor may tell you not to worry about trying to publish until your third year in the program, but students finishing their degrees and job hunting will tell you to begin submitting in your first year. You'll want to take advantage of the information sources that exist and compare notes on the answers you receive.

Graduate students. As I mentioned at the beginning of this chapter, other grad students are your best source for information about your program, since they can offer both extrinsic and intrinsic information. By spending time with students, you have the opportunity to ask the "dumb" questions you would be afraid to ask a professor, or delicate questions about your program and department that you can't ask anyone else.

Campus tour. You will gain the most from this kind of input by talking to grad students as early as possible. So, prior to registration, call the department and ask if a graduate student would be willing to tour the campus with you. If there is a graduate student organization at the university, it may have student members in your department whose duties include meeting with new students. You can find out about the existence of the organization from the department, the graduate office, or the student life office.

If you're married or have a family, request a student with similar circumstances. This suggestion also applies to disabled, international, minority, and women students. A guide with the same background as you can offer valuable insight. Obviously, a 23-year-old male student living in graduate housing is bound to have a different take on the program than a 40-year-old female student living off campus with her family.

If you're interested in the experiences of other graduate students as well, have lunch with a student or two. In such an informal setting, you'll get a variety of individual perspectives on graduate life. Also, newer

I received an orientation at the school I am presently attending. It was very formal and impersonal. It was intimidating! There were about sixty graduate students in a large room, sitting and staring at one another. No one was really sure what to do. The faculty introduced themselves to us—but no one gave the graduate students an opportunity to introduce themselves to the faculty. I found this very strange. I immediately wondered if the faculty actually cared about who we were. All in all, it was an omen to the type of environment that exists here: CHILLY.

—Darla, Ph.D. student, Sociology

students in the program may be aware of changes in university or departmental policy that don't apply to advanced students.

Meet the departmental staff. Your first stop on the tour should be the department itself, and you can begin by asking your student guide to introduce you to the departmental staff. The administrative assistants in the department are an invaluable source of information about departmental activities. Professors who are absorbed in research may only get piecemeal information regarding other faculty projects, but the AA's handle the entire department's administrative duties on a daily basis. AA's are also helpful in handling scheduling problems and answering questions about departmental procedures. Since the administrative staff is not typically involved in departmental politics, it can generally give unbiased reports on faculty members that can help you later in the program when you begin selecting an adviser and committee members. Request a listing of courses for the upcoming term from the AA's, and later in the tour you can review it with your student guide.

Meet the profs. The student guide may want you to meet his or her adviser or other available faculty members. Being introduced by another graduate student is a comfortable way to meet faculty members for the first time. Let the professors know that you're trying to get a head start on the program by meeting people and learning about the department. Professors respect initiative, and this first contact provides the foundation for informal relationships down the road. Remember that graduate school is an "apprenticeship" system and professors fully expect grad students to come to them for professional guidance. Faculty members will also appreciate your interest in their research, and you should offer to meet with them later on to discuss their current projects.

Meet other students. A student guide can also informally introduce you to other students in the student assistant office (the "mini-faculty lounge") or other departmental hub of activity. These places form the root of the graduate student grapevine because so many students congregate there in a relatively unsupervised environment. Introducing yourself to these students operates as a kind of preliminary networking because you may not see them later in the classroom. You will probably make friends with other new students you meet in classes, but those who have already completed their course work can give you valuable input on working with advisers or researching a dissertation.

Other sites on the tour. Once you've toured the department, the student can show you campus facilities like the library, bookstore, computer center, and recreation center. Find out where grad students hang out (when they find the time) and where the cheap restaurants are located. The university cafeteria may not be the only or best option for your budget. During the campus tour, ask about extrinsic issues such as the policies on insurance for students, taxes on financial aid, and any student discounts you are eligible to receive. You are probably eligible for free counseling services provided by the university, generally from psychology Ph.D. students as part of their internship. Grad students frequently report that they were unprepared as beginning students for the stress of the dissertation research process, but that counseling helped alleviate their anxiety. It's useful to know early on what services are available if you seek counseling later.

Asking the "sticky" questions. And finally, this is a good time, on a one-to-one basis, to find out about the faculty in the department. A senior student can provide the most valuable insights into how different professors work with their grad student advisees. Go over the course schedule with the student and ask about the personalities of the faculty teaching grad courses for your first term. You may want to inquire if their schedules allow them enough time to be effective thesis or dissertation advisers.

Find out about the level of funding professors receive for projects. If you're looking to get an RA, this information is particularly relevant. Who gets the best funding for RA's? How much work do these faculty members require of their RA's? You can ask about faculty politics, i.e., who's friends with whom, since this information will come in handy when you choose a thesis or dissertation committee.

OTHER STUDENTS ARE YOUR BEST SOURCES

A student guide can answer questions about your program that will prevent you from making costly mistakes. How soon do students select a thesis or dissertation topic? How soon do they begin trying to publish and present papers or posters at conferences? Do any of the professors have connections to professional journals?

> *It is especially critical for new graduate students to realize the difference between what's supposed to happen versus what really happens. Official orientation materials are, by their very nature, required to describe what's supposed to happen. Graduate students a couple of years older ("age" of course meaning length of time as a graduate student, not since birth) than you are your single best source of information on how things really get done.*
>
> *—Chris, Ph.D. student, Zoology*

Even if the student can't answer all of your questions, he or she can point you to students working with different advisers who would be willing to talk about their experiences.

Who's getting jobs and who's getting out? You can (and should) get information about job placement of students under different advisers from the department or the graduate office. The job placement of students working under different professors indicates not only the marketability of particular areas of research, but also whether professors have and use their connections to provide postgraduate opportunities for their students.

You can also get attrition rates of students from the same sources. You can do a little detective work on your own by checking which professors were advisers to the students who left the program. You should also try to find out about any discrimination against students under different faculty advisers.

Beyond the questions described above, you can get details about housing that the administration often doesn't provide. Over 80 percent of graduate students live on their own off campus, and another grad student can tell you where grad students in the department live and about the most affordable housing in the area. They can also describe from an insider's point of view which neighborhoods are the safest, "hip," most convenient, and so on.

INTERVIEWING FACULTY

Once the graduate students have given you some feedback about the department and faculty, you can seek out professors you think might be suitable as advisers for your area of interest. Let the professors know that you're thinking about pursuing a particular research interest and you'd like to know if it would be convenient for them to spend a few minutes talking with you in person about their areas of specialization.

BREAKING THE ICE WITH PROFS

Before meeting with a faculty member, see if you can obtain a copy of his or her curriculum vitae (CV), usually kept in the departmental files. The CV, basically an academic résumé, lists the professor's publications, and you can skim the most recent ones at the library to use as an introduction to his or her current research. When you first meet with the professor, the conversation may seem uncomfortable, or the professor may appear distracted. Treat this meeting like you would a first date: ask the professor about his or her own interests. Talk about the articles you've reviewed and ask how he or she got the ideas for the topics. Because faculty members spend the bulk of their time doing research, you'll most likely be asking about the very subject that's keeping them from concentrating on you. Another icebreaker is to ask a professor to point you to the best texts on a particular subject, along with any new or landmark articles you should be aware of in your field. You can then lead in to questions about the requirements he or she has for their research assistants. If the professor employs RA's, ask what kinds of work the RA's perform in the lab or in the library.

Common sense should tell you to keep the meeting brief unless the professor is engaged in discussing his or her research interests. Close the meeting by asking the professor to recommend a graduate student, perhaps an RA or TA, who might be willing to talk to you. The professor will appreciate the fact that you do not want to intrude further upon his or her time. Also, you can contact other students who work regularly with this faculty member and ask them to describe a typical "day in the life" of an RA or TA.

Although a face-to-face meeting is best, if you can't get to campus, see if you can schedule a phone conversation. Also, don't forget about e-mail. Students and professors may be more candid when using e-mail than when using the telephone. Get e-mail addresses from professors or the department. Keep the questions specific and fairly simple to answer until you get their responses. If they seem agreeable and interested in talking further, you can follow up with the more detailed questions. You may even want to use the e-mail correspondence to get noticed, and schedule a face-to-face meeting later when you're on campus.

BEWARE OF DISCRIMINATION

One unforeseen difficulty faced by new graduate students is the mistaken perception that inside the "Ivory Tower" discrimination is non-existent, that the academic environment encourages only liberal openness and tolerance. Regrettably, the truth is that universities are no less plagued by incidents of discrimination than any other workplace.

Be conscious of this reality, and don't allow your efforts as a graduate student to be compromised by selecting an inappropriate adviser.

Other graduate students with backgrounds similar to yours are the best source for information about the nuances of discriminatory behavior. Find out which faculty members encourage and support students with your background. After all, the choice of an adviser is under your control. For more about this issue in selecting an adviser and committee members, take a look at Chapter 8.

INTERVIEWING FACULTY

A professor's individual expectations of your progress should be an important indicator for you in deciding on an adviser. Ask about the time frame for beginning a thesis or dissertation and choosing a topic. Find out his or her expectations concerning conferences and publishing for grad students.

If you did not submit a writing sample to the professor during the initial application process, you may want to give him or her a sample of your work, particularly if it touches on the professor's area of expertise. The paper may not be read, or the professor may only flip to the back to check your references, but at the very least the paper remains on his or her desk and serves to keep you in mind.

As I stressed before, taking the initiative in meeting with professors before school begins will not draw negative attention to you. The effect is the reverse—you will be recognized early on by prospective advisers, and your enthusiasm about the program may eventually lead to better financial aid opportunities from professors seeking help with their research. In addition, meeting with faculty members is good practice for the dissertation process, when you will have to schedule meetings with your adviser and committee members on a regular basis.

LABORATORY

You can schedule a lab visit either through a graduate student or by asking a professor to introduce you to his or her lab group. Ideally, this visit should occur during the admissions process, particularly for students seeking RA positions. As a student in the sciences, the lab will become your home away from home, and the lab environment, including the attitudes of students among different lab groups, will influence your decision on which research interests to pursue.

ASSIGNED GRADUATE ADVISER

Some universities assign you a faculty adviser until you have selected your own. Because they are members of your department, these advisers can answer the extrinsic questions about your program of study and give you details on the degree requirements. They can likewise recommend courses to take as a beginning student and suggest time frames for picking a topic for your thesis or dissertation and selecting an adviser and committee members. Frequently, an assigned adviser can direct you to professors with research interests similar to your own. Many students I surveyed reported that their assigned advisers only offered rudimentary knowledge about the program, so you should definitely supplement the information they provide with advice from other other grad students and professors.

GRADUATE STUDENT ASSOCIATIONS

The graduate office, department, or student life office can tell you if there is an organization on campus devoted to grad student concerns. Some universities also have a minority graduate student organization. Most graduate student organizations offer an on-campus orientation. In addition, the association will usually have a handout or a guide that tells incoming students about the policies and procedures of the university, complete with a map of the campus and helpful hints on using campus facilities. These guides also offer information on housing and on the general area in which the campus is located, which you need to know before you move. One of the most valuable services provided by some associations is a TA handbook, targeted at incoming teaching assistants, which describes the basics of teaching for that particular university and usually includes helpful information about other students' experiences.

If you are still off campus, call the association and find out if there are graduate student members from your department and contact them. Any student in the grad student organization can answer general questions about graduate school, such as student discounts, taxes on financial aid, insurance, housing, and so on. The graduate student association can usually provide a list of graduate and professional organizations of which you can become a member as well as information about alumni career services.

LIBRARY AND COMPUTER CENTER

Both the library and computer center have full-time staff members to assist students, so you can take a supervised tour. You should not need to schedule this in advance, although you may want to call ahead to the library staff and find out if they arrange group tours. While touring the library, ask about particular reference sources available for graduate study in your field. Be sure to ask about special privileges for graduate students in borrowing books and using Special Collections or Interlibrary Loan services. Most libraries have lockers and study carrels designated for grad students, and a librarian can tell you how to get them.

Other Perks: Internet. Grad students often get special privileges at the computer center. If you don't yet have an Internet account, now is the time! Internet

WHEN YOU CAN'T DO A TOUR

If you can't get to campus to make an early reconnaissance, or haven't yet moved, you can still call the department for telephone numbers or e-mail addresses of grad students who would be willing to talk about the program. If you've already made contact with some of the professors in the department, you can ask them to recommend students to you.

The university scheduled a full-day orientation for us a week before classes began. The Graduate English Association also planned a reception for us to meet the students who are already there and the professors. The GEA is in charge of all of this, and it seems to be an excellent group. They sent out a sheet with the names and phone numbers of all the members, offering rides from the airport and enclosing a list of grad students who still needed roommates.

—Jennifer, Ph.D. student, English

access is usually free to students, and the sooner you get "netted," the sooner you can access specific kinds of research materials available on the Internet. My Internet access has offered opportunities I couldn't have gotten any other way: friendships with grad students outside of my university, advanced notice about upcoming publications and conferences, contact with distinguished scholars and editors of academic journals, and the sharing of ideas and bibliographic materials through on-line discussion groups. The computer center can tell you how to find and join graduate student and professional newsgroups.

If you're weak on using word processing programs, ask about courses provided by the computer center. For a nominal fee, the computer center usually conducts classes in everything from basic PC operations to conducting advanced Internet research. They may also sell computer equipment or tell you how to get it (usually through the bookstore), including any student discounts.

COURSE WORK AND EXAMS

I had a nightmare about my generals. In addition to the written and oral parts, there was a physical challenge. I remember a sumo wrestling ring of some sort, and you had to get in there and either just wrestle or beat the living daylights out of your opponent. I took this as a sign that I really needed to calm down!

—Joe, Ph.D. student, Metallurgy

Deadlines sneak up without warning, and it's an unfortunate fact that most of us don't think about the various hoops of our programs until we get ready to jump through them. When we're taking courses, we concentrate only on the courses; when we're studying for exams, we focus on exams. Because the next stage of the program seems to come out of nowhere, most students feel unprepared and anxious when it comes to finishing course work and studying for exams. But it doesn't have to be this way. Let "Be Prepared" become your mantra and you can jump through the hoops with a flourish!

BEFORE YOU SIGN UP

You will feel more prepared right off the bat if you take the time to find out the details of your program

One of the worst moments during my first year was trying to prepare for my comprehensive exams. In previous years, the comps were held in August, but for our group they were held in June. I talked to the head of graduate studies because I wanted to go home during that time to see my sister graduate from high school. I mentioned this conflict, and his response was, "How fast can you drive?" No matter how fast I drove, I couldn't do it. I passed both sets of comps, but the point I learned is that nothing comes above graduate school, not even your family.

—George, Ph.D. student, Economics

requirements. The course catalog or departmental brochure will list the requirements for completing your program of study, but these provide only a skeleton outline. For each stage of the degree—required course work, exams, selection of committees and adviser, thesis/dissertation proposal—the department provides detailed guidelines. You don't have to wait until you've completed your course work to get this information. Go to the departmental administrative assistants or graduate director and request copies of everything. Once you've looked over the information provided, you will have a clearer idea of what's expected of you at each level of the program. And you'll have a head start in understanding any bureaucratic channels or scheduling constraints surrounding the process.

It's a good idea to get a calendar and use it to keep track of the hours you spend working and studying. I didn't think of this until my second year in grad school, when I began studying for my comprehensive exam. But it has helped enormously since then in scheduling my work and keeping me productive. By tracking the hours I spend each day sitting in class, doing research in the library, working as an RA, or staring at my computer screen awaiting inspiration (or surfing the Net), I can see if I'm giving one project too much priority over others. It's also very gratifying at the end of a year's time to see that, yes, I have been working! Graduate school is no walk in the park and having this self-fashioned accounting for all your time and effort, especially in the absence of a bounteous paycheck or faculty pats on the back, will help relieve those periodic moments of doubt.

Course Work: "Intro to Departmental Politics"
Scheduling courses will be your first experience in navigating the murky waters of departmental politics. Don't use your undergraduate charts! It's not as simple as just signing up for a course that interests you or meets the requirements. At the graduate level, you need to be aware of the political and economic agendas behind the classes and the exam(s), as well as the status of professors involved in research projects. Many of the mistakes grad students make come from taking an undergraduate approach to scheduling classes and exams.

Dedication and a knowledge of your subject are not enough—you need street smarts now. The ultimate goal is to get the degree without spending time doing unnecessary research or wasting money. You are your own manager in this process.

For all disciplines, course work provides students with ideas about possible thesis/dissertation topics and introduces them to the level of scholarship required for their disciplines. Students may have an assigned faculty adviser until they choose one on their own, or they may work with the graduate director in selecting courses. Ask these professors about gearing your course work toward fulfilling the exam requirements and let them make suggestions. Be sure to balance this advice with student input, however, before you sign up.

USING COURSE WORK TO PASS EXAMS

While you're thinking about which classes to take, remember that course work is never an end unto itself. You want classes that also prepare you for the exams required to get your degree. Before you sign up for your first class, know the nature of the exam you will be taking and tailor your course work accordingly.

MAKING THE GRADE

Grade inflation is the norm in grad school, which means that failing a class or even getting a "C" is nonexistent. You're expected to get "A"s in your classes by the time you reach the graduate level, and faculty members tend to give out "A"s even though students have different standings. In most cases, a "B" in a class indicates that something went wrong. A student may have turned in work past a deadline, misread instructions for an assignment, or had a personality conflict with the professor. Sometimes a professor doesn't agree with a student's perspective and will interpret this conflict as an intellectual deficiency rather than a matter of judgment.

Some students suggest that you begin your program by taking the easiest classes first. Those who started out with a "killer" class—one with a heavy workload or a demanding professor—say that they were forced to do extra work to build their reputations as strong students, and a few complain that they were never able to establish themselves as good students. By talking with other grad students, you'll have an idea of the difficulty level of courses offered, including the workload expected by the instructor. If you do well right from the start, you won't have to work as hard later to establish a good reputation in the department.

A WORD ABOUT INCOMPLETES

Think of an incomplete as a Trojan Horse—it looks like a gift but in reality it promises ruin. And don't be fooled by the fact that taking incompletes in course work is common at the graduate level; it's still not a good alternative to finishing the course. Sometimes students, pressured by the more immediate duties of research or teaching, may put off course work to the point that they are unprepared to finish the class. Incompletes may or may not show up on your transcript—if they do, it's a strike against you in the job search. An incomplete may buy some time, but it has other drawbacks (see Dottie's Story below). It makes more sense to try to finish classes as you take them. You have no way of knowing what your schedule will look like down the road. Don't bet on your future.

DOTTIE'S STORY

Until she took an incomplete in a class, Dottie had a 4.0 GPA in her classes. Feeling overwhelmed with her first year of grad school, dealing with family matters, and beginning a new job, she decided to take an incomplete in one of her classes, hoping to have more time once things got settled. But while deferring the class seemed like a good idea at the time, she found that, as the months progressed, she had even less time to spend on finishing the course requirements. She was already taking another semester of classes and her job duties were getting more demanding, not less. By the time the second deadline came around for the course, she realized—too late—that she had a heavier workload now than ever before. She worked over her Christmas break to try to get the course requirements finished and let her other course work get behind. All that work, and she still got a "B"!

YOUR EXAMINATIONS COMMITTEE

For all of your graduate exams, an examinations committee is either assigned or selected by you. In some cases, the examinations committee becomes a student's dissertation committee. These committees have different levels of involvement in preparing their students. In the sciences and social sciences, the committee will typically be more active in helping the student tailor courses toward fulfilling the exam requirement, making suggestions for readings and offering potential or actual study questions. In the humanities, the committee may work with a student to prepare a reading list of materials from which exam questions will be taken. Some committees welcome questions from students about potential exam topics—other committees forbid discussion entirely, leaving students to study on their own. By looking at the detailed departmental handouts, you will know what level of involvement you can expect from your own committee.

LENGTH OF EXAMS

The length will vary depending on the school and program, but the most common form requires that students take a series of tests over the course of several days. One 8-hour test may be offered on Monday, with the next on Tuesday covering a different topic, and so on. Study time also varies depending on the material tested. Students most commonly report needing a three-month study period to prepare. Because it's standard for exams to be offered in the fall, students will spend the summer months preparing. A few students I interviewed spent only one evening studying for their tests—a few spent as long as two years! Talking to students in your department who have successfully completed their exams will be the best indicator of when to begin scheduling your study time. Don't wait for classes to be finished before you begin thinking about the exam. At the beginning of your program, mark an estimated date in your calendar to select a committee, if applicable, or to begin gathering study materials. The

EXAM LINGO

For new students, sometimes just the terminology of grad-level exams is disconcerting. What's the difference between comps, quals, and orals?

Because the types of exams vary so much from department to department and from school to school, your program may have its own specialized jargon, but here are the basic explanations.

Comps or *generals*, comprehensive or general exams, typically are the exams you take after completing your course work. This type of exam may have both written and oral components, although it's more common at this early stage for the exam to be in written form. As suggested by the name, these exams cover the whole discipline, and questions are usually taken from required or suggested course work. M.A. students only have to fulfill this single exam requirement to get their degrees.

Ph.D. students generally face a second set of exams. *Quals* or *prelims*, qualifying or preliminary exams, refer to the second set of exams required for a student to proceed to the dissertation. These exams more often have an *oral* component and test the student's specialized knowledge of a field. By this later point in the program, students should have selected an area of specialization within their fields. This exam tests one's competency in pursuing a dissertation in a particular subject area.

date may change, but at least you'll have a reminder and won't be caught by surprise with an approaching deadline.

GRADING EXAMS

Exams are graded as pass/fail. Some schools offer an "A+" on the exam in the form of a Pass with Distinction or a High Pass. Keep in mind that getting this "A+" requires a substantial investment of your time. If you want to go for the gold, make sure folks outside your department will know it, either from your transcripts or in letters of recommendation from your faculty. Balance the prestige of a High Pass with other projects that can increase your reputation inside and outside the department—presenting a paper at a conference, shaping up a paper for publication, or networking.

TYPES OF EXAMS

There are a bewildering array of exam formats. The individual requirements for your program may not resemble any of these approaches below or may be a combination of several. In addition, these formats may be offered at the masters or doctoral level. I've provided some general strategies for taking exams. But since students who have taken the exams are the best source for strategies, I've included more student quotes in this chapter than in any other. Exams may incorporate any of the following, sometimes in combination.

- Course work
- Reading list
- Portfolio
- Research paper
- Literature review
- Grant proposal (see Chapter 7)
- Exam topics based on faculty research interests
- Exam topics based on student's major and minor fields of specialization
- Student defines topics with the approval of the exam committee
- Oral exam as general presentation/lecture
- Oral exam as defense of research proposal (see Chapter 7)

- Oral exam as explanation of written exam responses
- Foreign language exam or equivalent research skills

FOREIGN LANGUAGE EXAMS: ¿QUÉ PASA?

The foreign language exam sounds more intimidating than it really is. I panicked when I did my first go-round with grad school applications, assuming (erroneously) that I would have to read Horace's *Ars Poetica* in the original Latin for my first class assignment. In reality, meeting this requirement in the humanities usually involves taking undergrad language courses once you get into the program. These classes may count toward your graduate GPA, but, ironically, may not be credited to the hours you need for your degree. Take a look at your program requirements again and find out if a "B" in these classes will go on your transcript.

Graduate prep courses. Aside from undergrad classes, many schools offer a fantastic grad-level prep course designed to help you pass the language requirement. Fortunately, these classes bypass the conversational element of undergraduate language courses—no "Yes, it is foggy and cold today" or "Where is the American Express office?" in these courses. Just the basics you need to pass the exam: grammar, verb tenses, and a little vocabulary. In most cases you're allowed to bring a dictionary (and sometimes a grammar book) into the foreign language exam. You will be given a passage to translate, either from a newspaper or magazine. The passage may also be related to an academic topic. The exam does not test your speech fluency—just your reading knowledge of a language. You will not be sitting down with Professor Medici to discuss Renaissance mercantile practices in fluent Italian, so don't panic.

Exemption from the foreign language requirement. Some programs will exempt you from the foreign language requirement if you have taken two years or

For my exam I picked up a few extra books that might give me an outside perspective on the topics that interest my committee members. One member of my committee spends a lot of her research time on ecological theory, so I'm reading a book of fundamental papers to get a good background in the kinds of things that interest her. It's not so much catering to the professors as trying to be prepared for any curve balls they might throw.

—Jack, M.S. student, Biology

more of a foreign language as an undergraduate. You may, however, be required to take a placement test prior to enrollment to ensure that your level of competence in the language meets the program standards. But an exam committee may waive this requirement depending on whether or not foreign language fluency relates to your research interests. Science and social science departments have all but eliminated the foreign language requirement, substituting it instead with "research methods" courses more directly related to the discipline. Common substitutions include classes in research methods, statistics, and computer science.

PREPARING FOR EXAMS: AN EXERCISE IN SOCIAL DARWINISM

The exams will probably be your first experience of intense competition with your peers. Obviously, there are positive and negative aspects of this competition. The plus side on a personal level is that you'll find yourself pushing harder for the exam than you have for any of the other requirements. Professionally, you'll really start to dig into your area of study and, like many students, you may find this concentrated study of your field rewarding. The down side is that the competition can isolate you from other students, many of whom are great sources of information. Take care of Number One, but try also to maintain a healthy balance between personal satisfaction and academic success.

Take classes with committee members. One general strategy to psych out what might be on the exam is to take classes with professors who are on the examinations committee. This is a great way to get an idea of the committee's particular research interests and testing methods. Questions related to faculty research have a mysterious way of popping up on exams. A few schools actually test their students' knowledge of faculty research projects. And, taking classes with professors on the exam committee allows you to prove yourself to a professor in a less stressful environment. Name-dropping is very common in the classroom: know who professors regard highly and check out their research at the library. Look at the scholars a professor cites in his or her own research. And know who they dislike. You don't want to cite researchers that committee members regard as incompetent or unreliable.

The same thing goes for selecting your examinations committee. If you can select your committee, you have a great opportunity to pass with distinction. You can choose faculty members who are already impressed with your work. You can also become familiar with their expectations for the exam. Ask them about potential exam questions, research you should be aware of, and the theory behind the test. Does the exam test your ability to think creatively? Does it test general or specialized knowledge? Are you supposed to solve a problem or quote sources? Should you know current research, landmark research, or both?

To do well you'll need to know more than the topics covered—you need to know how you're supposed to cover them. The key is to know the philosophy behind the questions, and if you have selected your committee, you're in much better shape to get that information without having to guess.

In *Getting What You Came For*, Robert Peters suggests that you write up a list of exam questions, with answers, and ask your adviser to review them. The adviser can spot gaps by having actual samples of your work, and his or her recommendations will be more substantial. Hey, who knows? Maybe your adviser will subconsciously absorb this material and ask you similar questions.

Write up class notes related to the exam. As you take classes, begin thinking of potential exam questions related to the course content. Once you've completed a course, it's a good idea to create a synopsis of the material covered vis-á-vis the material outlined on the syllabus. Make note of a professor's emphasis of particular material while the knowledge is still fresh in your mind. This approach will save you study time later when you review your notes.

Organize your notes. If you're working with a reading list or collating sources for a literature review, develop a method for cataloging and summarizing your readings. I prefer using the computer, but some students use flash cards or index cards. There are a variety of note-taking computer applications available—you can invest in one now and take more advantage of it later when you're

DEPARTMENT MATERIALS

Many times previous exams are available in the department as study guides. The first thing to know before you get started is whether or not the same committee that designed the old exams will be designing yours. Assigned exam committees rotate, and you may be looking at a test developed by last year's committee—but not this year's.

Departmental assistants may also have notes, reading lists, or other study materials on file. Know what a Pass with Distinction looks like. With these study guides and input from professors, you'll be much more confident about the material.

compiling thesis/dissertation research. Recommendations from students include FileMaker Pro, EndNote, Memory Mate, FoxPro, WordCruncher, and, for putting notes in hypertext format, WordPerfect 6.0 (and later versions) and HyperCard.

Besides including the meaty points from the readings, add possible exam questions that might come from the readings. You may see connections in the books and articles that you won't see later when you're reviewing your notes. While the material is fresh in your mind, jot down any connections between one source and another and any recurring themes or patterns. If you get to select a reading list with your committee, pay attention to who recommends what. Just by knowing their selections you'll have an idea of what these committee members will ask during the exam.

Use the exam to prepare for your thesis/dissertation. If your exam includes submitting a research paper, one good approach is to select a topic related to future thesis/dissertation research. Some programs even require the paper to be related in this way. The paper can yield great "pregame" feedback on your topic and initiate faculty enthusiasm. Conversely, if a committee has problems with it, you'll know to change your focus or, if you want to stick with it, at least select a thesis/dissertation committee that's more in tune with your interests.

The key when choosing a paper topic is to think ahead. What can the paper do for you in addition to meeting the exam requirement? Can it be an effective stepping-stone for future projects? For example, if you plan to finish school after getting a master's and go to work, you may want to select a topic that will get the attention of a future employer—a topic less academic in scope but appealing to industry or corporate executives.

Form a study group. And, finally, one of the best ways to prepare for your exam is studying with other students. My study group was the best part of my comps. I had a tighter bond with the group members than with any other students in the program. In part, this was because we shared a common experience. But it was also because we acted as a support group for each other during a very stressful period.

Working in a study group introduces you to the hands-on process of collaboration. You will be amazed how much this input from others will enhance your grasp of a topic. Most times study groups will divide up the work being covered so that one student writes up the major points on one topic for all of the other members. This may sound like an unreliable method, but all of the students in the group share not only a desire to pass but also a responsibility to the other members to be thorough in their research. You will find that in most cases students take this latter responsibility very seriously and will spend more time on preparation than they would if they were going it alone.

One tricky part of such a group work is the individual decision to keep or withhold insights, or "hoarding the intellectual gold." You may want to save a juicy bit of analysis to make yourself look better on the exam rather than contributing it to the group knowledge.

This dynamic occurred early on in my group, mainly because we knew we were in direct competition with each other. But a funny thing happened as the meetings continued: everyone's defenses gradually broke down and we all wound up sharing insights about the readings and offering information for the benefit of the whole group. It is a difficult decision under this kind of pressure to be a collaborator rather than a Lone Star.

As a result of our individual choices to take on an active teaching role, however, we all did very well on the exam. And the level of excitement and satisfaction we had for the other members was higher than it would have been if we'd kept our insights to ourselves.

Schedule mock exams. Even if you're working outside of a formal group, you should share your class notes with other students. Students have a habit of taking notes only on topics that catch their interest. Comparing your perspective on relevant topics with others will help eliminate any gaps. If a professor showed enthusiasm for a student's paper or exam in a class, take a look at it to see what makes it tick.

Mock exams are another great way to prepare for the biggie. Find out where on campus the exam will be given and go over to the examinations room and practice taking tests there. Just seeing the dreaded room that holds your future in the balance will help you to

STUDY GROUP TIPS

When you first meet with your group, set a schedule right away for weekly or biweekly meetings, and make sure to get together more often as the exam date approaches. You'll need each other then! Decide who's covering what areas, and how you want the information condensed and distributed to the other members.

Keep the meeting place and time consistent. And take a break occasionally to grab a beer together or go out to dinner. Find out where your fellow students grew up, what their parents or spouses do, how old their kids are. This group may be the only personal life you have for several months, and despite having different backgrounds (or because of it) you may make friends you'll keep forever.

HONE YOUR PUBLIC SPEAKING SKILLS

Many students say that teaching experience made their orals less terrifying. Teaching won't eliminate nervousness entirely, but you'll get invaluable practice in thinking on your feet. If you don't have this option, you may want to invest in taking a public speaking course, or join a group such as Toastmasters that will help improve your skills for free.

The classroom is ideal preparation, however, for the type of exam you will be taking. You get practice answering questions and asking them, and your students will be a good gauge of any distracting mannerisms or habits. Just watch how they're watching you.

overcome some of the test-day jitters. This goes for both oral and written exams. My university has an unwritten policy that rooms must be subzero during the summertime and sweltering in the winter. Checking out the room beforehand helped us know what we should wear to be more comfortable.

Get together with other students, write up sample questions, oral or written, and drill, drill, drill. Your fellow students are excellent "pre-profs," and they can offer constructive criticism and effective tips for improving your writing or speaking. If you do this in the test environment you'll breeze in on exam day with fewer surprises. You can also hold mock exams with just one other student, with an understanding spouse or significant other, or alone if you're not working with a group.

Videotape yourself. Using a videotape recorder is a very effective way to prepare for oral exams. Have another student ask you a sample exam question and tape yourself responding. For some students the idea of watching themselves on video rivals major dental surgery, but it's the best way to know how you come across to others. You'll be a little nervous if you haven't taught before or have only seen yourself in a less-than-flattering driver's license photo. But you'll find that the nervousness of having the camera trained on you will fade as you begin thinking about your answers. While playing back the tape, pay attention to body language and habits that attract attention away from what you're saying. It may be that you've always wanted to quit biting your nails or your lip—now is the time! Expressing yourself with your hands is great, but wild gesticulations make you look like an out-of-control aircraft spinning rapidly toward earth.

Listen to your speech as well. Many people were raised to regard silence as an awkward moment in conversation and will try to fill up gaps with meaningless chatter. Try being silent a few moments if you need to pause for breath or you want a second to think. The first lesson that high-priced speaking consultants teach is to substitute a brief "thoughtful pause" every time you want to say "um" or "you know." If you want to sound more articulate, replace every "um" with "as I understand it," "what became clear to me," or "and this was really interesting" or even rephrase the question. And remember that "like" is a preposition, not an all-purpose interjection. Try to speak strongly. Instead of beginning your responses with, "Well, I think that . . ." say, "As I was doing research on this topic I discovered that . . ." Try to make your segues sound less like a desperate grab for time and more like a formal introduction to your topic, and practice on tape or in the mirror until your speech sounds smooth and mature.

WHAT HAPPENS IF YOU BLOW IT?

It does happen, more often than you think. Very bright students will fail their exams for a number of reasons. A good student in my program failed his comps because he dared to condemn the texts and authors he was tested on, an obvious no-no because the faculty had selected the works. It's only natural to expect that the faculty will pick topics or texts based on their own passions. So don't shoot yourself in the foot while trying to impress a committee with your wit and perception. Some creativity is, of course, required. But save the more digressive reflections for your Great American Novel. Play it safe for now.

If you should fail your exams, don't panic. It doesn't mean grad school is over for you. Most programs give you two chances to pass. Unless you get a hint that they're trying to drum you out of the program, most committees will not fail you the second time. In fact, they will probably be motivated to discuss problems with your approach, research, or writing and offer suggestions for improvement. Often, the first failure doesn't show up on your transcript; some schools only include the Pass, indicating that you met the requirement. If so, great. Only your department will know and you can work to improve your standing with extra hard work.

The most painful experience in my entire life was failing my oral comps the first time around. I think I just burned out. I got very intimidated by my committee members, and I wasn't used to saying my answers out loud or writing them on a blackboard. It was excruciating for all involved. I had never in my life failed anything so thoroughly.

I took them again later, and I worked hard for it. I had practice sessions with my adviser and lab mates. It was a real turning point in my life. My attitude toward my committee is much different now—I think of them as colleagues rather than superiors.

—Vicky, Ph.D. student, Environmental Science

TEACHING

Introverts, take a deep breath and prepare yourselves. You're going to be teaching as part of your academic training—unless you have a full non-service fellowship. For most students, teaching becomes a larger part of their lives as they approach the completion of their degrees. Doctoral students usually need the extra bucks from teaching to fund them through the writing of their dissertations. No sooner have they finished with their own classes than they find themselves back in the classroom teaching undergrads.

In most cases, the teaching requirement is part of a student's financial aid package. Students may not be required to teach until after they've completed their course work, but it's not uncommon for schools to require students to teach shortly after they start their program. In particular, large, state-funded schools need the help to teach seminar classes for lower-division students. One school reported that 90 percent of its lower-division courses are taught by graduate TA's.

Some students granted a teaching assistantship may actually be "assistants," subordinate to a professor in a large class. Other students will be totally in charge of their own classrooms. It really depends on the size of the undergraduate population and the university's financial situation. A large state school, with an eye always toward cutting costs and stretching resources, will prefer cheaper student labor to the cost of hiring more faculty.

Attitudes about teaching vary tremendously from student to student. It's more common for grad students in the pure sciences to resent their teaching responsibilities—many of them will go on to jobs outside of academe and feel that teaching skills are not relevant to their career goals. Students who plan on staying in the Ivory Tower, however, generally find teaching to be a rewarding personal experience and an invaluable professional skill. For some students, teaching is the best part of their graduate training. It's true that teaching takes time away from research and class preparation, but it also keeps grad students up-to-date on their own world. Undergrads keep grad students grounded (for better or worse!) in the larger cultural life outside academe.

TEACHING YOUR WAY TO A BETTER CAREER

If you know that a teaching assistantship will be part of your training, you can use the experience to enhance other aspects of your graduate career. Serving as a TA for a potential adviser is a great way to know how you will interact on a thesis/dissertation. Working as a TA may also provide you with ideas about a professor's research that you can expand into a thesis/dissertation topic. Teaching undergrad courses can be an excellent brush-up on general knowledge of your field. In fact, many students use their assistantships to teach classes that will help them get ready for their exams. If you're lucky enough to teach a class in your specialty, the extra reading for class preparation, in addition to the readings you do for graduate classes, may give you thesis/dissertation ideas before you begin doing the official research.

PREPARING TO TEACH

Your university may not have a formal TA training program in place. A surprising number of schools just

Your first year, try to teach courses that will help you with upcoming departmental exams. After that, become a TA for professors you might wish to work with down the road or concentrate on courses in which you want to develop your expertise. Teaching not only makes you learn material well but it also provides great fodder for dissertation work.
—Lorraine, Ph.D. student, English

Here are the first questions
you should ask about your
class, according to the University of Georgia TA manual:

- Are the course schedule, syllabus, textbook, and format decided by the department?

- Has the classroom been reserved?

- Have the textbooks been ordered?

- Has the library been notified of books to be put on reserve?

- Will you use standard department tests or design your own?

throw you into the classroom without any training at all. Fortunately, many schools publish their TA handbooks, so they're available to TA's at other schools. You can check them out from the library. These handbooks, from such schools as Northwestern, Berkeley, Stanford, and Indiana, cover everything a new instructor needs to know before he or she teaches the first class. If your school does not offer a TA training program, you can still talk with other students who have taught classes to get their input. An informative guide for schools and students interested in forming a TA program is *Preparing Graduate Students To Teach*, edited by Leo M. Lambert and Stacy Lane Tice. This book, also listed in the annotated bibliography, highlights successful TA training programs from various schools and disciplines.

As soon as you have been assigned to teach or assist in an undergrad class, you need to begin preparing for it. This first teaching experience will take the most time (it gets easier as you go along). You don't want to add the anxiety of poor preparation to the inevitable nervousness of facing 30 to 100 expectant strangers for the first time. The best way to minimize the stress of teaching your first class is to have the administrative details covered well in advance.

You'd be surprised to know how often it is up to the TA to take care of these administrative details. Don't expect the process to be handled magically by someone else. If you know you will be assisting a professor, get together with him or her as soon as you can and go over the following points (adapted from the Berkeley TA handbook):

1. What should take place in discussion or lab meetings and how can these meetings be integrated with lectures?
2. What responsibilities will I have for student evaluations and grading?
3. How much freedom will I have to present materials not specifically addressed or to experiment with the classroom format?
4. How many office hours will I hold? Where is the office space for TA's?
5. Have there been any difficulties with the course in previous years?

6. Does the professor plan to meet with TA's during the semester to discuss the progress of the course or any problems TA's may be having?
7. How do I obtain course readings? (TA's can sometimes get free copies of books, and should check with the bookstore to ensure books will arrive on time.)
8. Have the course description and syllabus been prepared?
9. What is the maximum number of students the professor wants in each section? What should I do if attendance exceeds this number?

KNOW UNIVERSITY POLICIES AND PROCEDURES

Don't spend too much time grading student papers! Students can only remember three major comments on a paper anyway—don't bleed on their papers. It will eat up your life.

—Brent, Ph.D. student, English

Another important part of the TA process at your school is becoming familiar with policies and procedures. You're being paid for your assistantship, so you should know the university's employment and taxation policies. You'll need to know when you get paid. TA's sometimes get a nasty surprise when their regular paychecks are is stopped during the summer, or when the payment schedules abruptly change. All of the regulations are in print somewhere, and you can't appeal to the university administration if you failed to read them. Usually, you will have to apply to renew your assistantship, so you need to know the process for reapplying, including any deadlines, well in advance.

TA's often get added student benefits, but schools can be very tight-lipped about informing you of these perks. You may be eligible now for special parking privileges, health insurance, free interlibrary loan service, library locker or study carrel, free copying in the department, assistance from departmental AA's, and/or student discounts at the bookstore. Most schools also provide a teaching resource center to help you get started. The center offers information on past courses (including syllabi and schedules), audiovisual check-out services, assistance with library services, and clubs and organizations related to grad student teaching. If your privileges are not listed anywhere, ask around—more experienced TA's will know what services they're entitled to.

In addition, you need to know about the services offered to undergrad students on campus. Find out about the facilities for academic assistance and tutoring—hours, location, and any restrictions. Other helpful services include personal counseling, the language lab, career planning and placement, student groups, and disabled student programs. Before you walk into your first class you should already be familiar with the university policy on academic honesty and the process of addressing student grievances.

BALANCING TEACHING AND COURSE WORK

With this information in hand, you can begin to think about scheduling your time for the course. Many students recommend that you do not take a full graduate course load while you're teaching, particularly if it's your first class. Many schools will allow TA's to maintain their status as full-time students regardless of their course load. At others, dropping to half-time status can affect your external sources of support, or exclude you from certain university services. So find out how a course load change will affect your status.

To balance your time with other responsibilities, devote specific days of the week solely to teaching, grading, drafting exams, and so on, and other days to thesis/dissertation research, lab work, and preparation for your graduate classes. If you're not careful, you'll give too much time to the "no-brainer" administrative details of teaching just to avoid the thinking and planning of your own research. It's a sure way of prolonging your time to degree.

YOUR COURSE SCHEDULE AND SYLLABUS

Now you can get down to the nitty-gritty. Begin by thinking about what you want to accomplish in the course. Make a list of course objectives. What do you want students to know? Read the text and decide how best to cover the material to meet these objectives. Studies show that undergrad students, particularly freshmen and sophomores, feel uncomfortable if an instructor omits a substantial portion of the material or jumps around the textbook. If the text is assigned but you don't like its organization or content (and this is not uncommon), include additional readings that will help students get more out of the required text, but try to stick to a 1-2-3 approach with the text itself.

When you're working on the course schedule, make sure the dates for grading student assignments and tests do not conflict with your own deadlines for other projects such as research, graduate classwork, and holidays. For those days when you know you will be swamped with other graduate responsibilities, you can schedule films, guest lecturers, or fieldwork to minimize preparation.

The department will usually have guidelines for attendance already; there may even be a university-wide policy. In most cases you can also obtain departmental guidelines on exams or samples to give you an idea of different formats. If the department doesn't provide this, find other TA's and get their samples. Or you can request input from faculty members who have taught the same course.

The key to a successful class schedule is to vary the format. For lower division courses you're required to cover tons of material in a very short time, so you may decide a lecture format is the best approach to quickly get through the information. A little variety in the schedule, however, is a welcome relief both to you and the students. If you're in charge of the class, or your professor has given you the go-ahead to experiment with the format, plan days for films, slides, TV programs,

PREPARING YOUR SYLLABUS

The ideal syllabus contains the following information (adapted from the Indiana University TA handbook):

- Instructor's name; office address, phone, and hours; course name/number; meeting time/place; and course texts
- Policy statement on grading, late or missed work, attendance, make-up work, and exams
- Statement of requirements: papers/assignments, discussion sections, lab sections, fieldwork
- Course calendars: course schedule/topic outline, assignment/lab/exam schedule

or other electronic media. Have guest lecturers. And include time for Q&A sessions and discussion.

RECORDING GRADES

You'll need to keep track of grades, obviously. Even though you'll get a copy of the roll from the registrar, you'll probably want to use some other method to record grades. Many TA's use spreadsheet programs like Lotus or Excel. A variety of shareware computer grade books are also available on the World Wide Web. If you choose, you can also track grades on a standard word processor or use the old-fashioned paper method.

And finally, before the first day arrives, visit the classroom you've been assigned and make sure there are no problems. The classroom size should match the expected number of students for the course. Check that the lighting is adequate and temperature comfortable, and find out if the room is equipped for audiovisual materials.

YOUR FIRST DAY

You'll be nervous. It's okay—the students will be, too. Don't use the ancient advice of picturing your audience in their underwear (this can only be distracting!). You are prepared—lecture notes at the ready. You arrived at the classroom early to make sure the door was unlocked, there was plenty of chalk, an eraser. If you want to change the seating arrangement, go for it. On the first day, students will want to see that you are: a) enthusiastic about the subject and willing to work; b) objective and fair; and c) sympathetic toward their concerns. You can start by introducing yourself to the students, and right away offer to meet with them during office hours or by appointment. If you wish you can give students your e-mail address; some TA's will also give out their home phone numbers and designated hours for calling. If the class size isn't unwieldy, try to schedule at least one consultation with each student during the term. You may also want to tell students a little bit about yourself, although it should tend toward the professional rather than the personal. You might outline your research interests and describe what you're working on at the moment.

Once they know a little about you, get to know a little about them. I recommend passing out index cards and asking students to list their name; class (freshman, sophomore, etc.); major (if applicable); other classes they're taking; and personal interests or hobbies. I also request that employed students write down what they do and how many hours per week they work.

Go over the syllabus. Afterward, pass out the syllabus and go over it line by line. Let students know they can ask questions while you're going through it. Once that's done, usually after 10 to 20 minutes, it's up to you to decide how to spend the rest of the class period. Many professors dismiss students after going over the syllabus the first day. If you know you have a lot of material to cover, you can jump right in (keeping in mind that many students may not have bought the texts yet). Alternately, you may want to discuss the overview of the course contents, what will be covered and, more importantly, why you're covering it. Your students may be shy the first day, but you can try to involve them in determining the class objectives. Ask them what they want out of the course and why they decided to take it.

Give a diagnostic test. Having the students take a diagnostic test will help you find out their levels of expertise in the subject matter. While this exercise probably won't thrill the students, it could be very useful to you as a new instructor. A diagnostic test will give you a sense of the technical level you can approach in the lectures. Some undergrads have complained that TA's go over their heads during lectures. You may garner better evaluations down the road by knowing up front how familiar students are with the topic. Keep in mind that the class culture is set early in the term. If the class will be geared toward discussion and interaction, start right away. If the students will be doing a lot of writing, begin with writing assignments as soon as possible.

FIRST CLASS

To alleviate the first-day jitters, chat with the students who show up early. Ask them how many classes they've taken in this subject, if they're thinking of majoring in it, what their other courses are, whether they work, and so on.

Write your name, office location and hours, and course name/number on the board.

Start the class on time—it sets a good example for the future and shows the students you respect their time. For undergrads nothing is more irritating than having to wait for an instructor to show up!

CONDUCTING LAB SESSIONS

Lab sessions require a few additional steps of preparation. Before you begin to teach in the lab, take a look at the lab space and make sure you know where all the materials are located. For each lab exercise, be familiar with the lesson students are supposed to get out of it. Know the theory on which the experiment is based. And do the entire experiment in advance! You may be a little rusty in basic lab skills.

For your first lab session, review the safety procedures and demonstrate them to the students. Show students where the equipment is located and let them know what to do if something goes wrong. Stress to them early on to clean up when they're done—the laboratory is not for them alone. As students begin working, walk around and let them know you're available if they have questions. Resist the temptation to do the experiment for them. Try to lead students through the problem so they can see their own mistakes and correct them.

GENERAL TEACHING TIPS

Be conscious of your use of language in the classroom. Do you have a gender-neutral vocabulary? In my graduate courses, whenever a professor uses the word *mankind* the whole class cringes, male and female. Avoid stereotyping: doctors, lawyers, astronauts, and politicians can be women; nurses, administrative assistants, and schoolteachers can be men. In addition, your students will come from all different backgrounds. Try not to focus on examples drawn from only one ethnic culture.

And, most importantly, treat your students as adults. Many times you will have older students in the classroom, working students, and students with family responsibilities. At first both you and these students may feel awkward, especially if a student is twenty years your senior. You're still the expert on the material, however. If you take them seriously they will be enthusiastic to hear what you have to say.

LECTURING

If all you do in your lecture is cover the reading assignments, students will quit reading them. Highlight only the important points from the reading. Your students will learn how to read the material by observing your points of emphasis in the text. Try to use the blackboard for a little variety.

Practice at home. If you've never lectured before, or have only read aloud from papers, you may want to practice at home beforehand. Speak for 20 minutes off the top of your head to see what it feels like. For many grad students it's a little disconcerting at first. You're not getting any feedback, and you have no idea how to segue smoothly from one topic to another. You may even want to videotape yourself to see how many "ums" and "you knows" come up in your speech, or whether you have any distracting mannerisms.

Summarize. Students will feel much more comfortable if you summarize the material at various points. I never get irritated by the undergrad mantra, "Are we gonna be tested on this?" I was a grade-hound when I was in college, and I bet I'm not the only one who ended up in grad school. Let your students know which material is important—you're never giving away the test, trust me! At the end of the class period, summarize the lecture, and let them know what will be covered next time.

DISCUSSION

One point that all TA manuals cover is the amount of time you should pause after asking students a question. Most new TA's never wait long enough—the recommended time is between 20 and 30 seconds. Try asking a question out loud at home and waiting 30 seconds. It's going to seem like a long time to you at first, but students will be using that time to think about the question and formulate their responses.

How to ask questions. The Indiana University TA handbook has suggestions for ways to ask questions in a specific manner. Use "what" instead of "why" when introducing a discussion topic. For example, instead of asking a broad or vague question, "Why do you think the Great Depression occurred?" ask them, "What circumstances led to the Great Depression?" This format allows everyone to contribute separate points without directly

I have taught both general and advanced courses. As for balancing the work, it comes down to remembering the purpose of graduate school. I am here to get an advanced degree and the teaching cannot consume me in the process.

—David, Ph.D student, Chemistry

As a TA, you may want to
assign a student to take notes
for each class. That student
would be responsible for
recording notes on the lecture
and reading them back at the
beginning of the next class.

This exercise will not only
make the minute-taker pay
more attention to the lecture,
but will also train students to
be better note-takers.

contradicting other students. It also yields concrete information that you can summarize, in list form, on the board.

Role-playing. Another provocative question format is to ask students to place themselves in the role of a famous historical figure: "If you were Malcolm X, would you agree or disagree with the Plessy v. Ferguson decision of 'separate but equal' and why?" or "How would Machiavelli/Simone de Beauvoir/Rush Limbaugh answer this question?" Not only do the students begin to see that there are often different "right" answers, but they will also recognize that the topics covered in class have impact across historical periods.

Discussion groups. Whether or not you have a large class, one effective discussion method is to break the class down into smaller groups to work on a problem. Write a statement or problem on the board and ask students to come up with a set of responses. You may want to give each group a subproblem to work on, and then come back together as a class to resolve the larger problem. For example, students in an English novel class may break up into groups to discuss different characters of a novel. Then the class as a whole discusses these characters in relation to the novel's action and plot structure. One person from the group can act as the spokesperson. In a large class this approach helps students get to know each other, and for shy students it allows them to participate in a less intimidating environment. You might assign the spokesperson role to students who participate less in class discussions. It may be easier for those students to report collective findings rather than their own.

Quiet students. As the course progresses, you will undoubtedly have students who consistently raise their hands and those who never make a contribution. To even out the class participation, one teaching authority recommends that you ask students to write down the answer to a question and then call on them to read their responses. Encouraging quiet students in this way boosts their confidence. If you aren't able to completely draw them out, however, don't worry about it. Some students just don't talk—it doesn't mean that they don't enjoy the class discussion or the topics covered. You'll often be surprised after the first exam how well these quiet students are responding to the course material. Sitting back and absorbing information works, too.

Chatty students. Occasionally students will treat a discussion period like group therapy, using it as an opportunity to air intensely personal views or grievances. I remember one undergrad class in which a student reacted to a Keats poem by saying, "It makes me feel like a numb animal crawling!" While the experience of poetry was undoubtedly cathartic for the student, the rest of the class may be wondering how the comment relates to a discussion of poetic form. (Or, more specifically, how an animal can crawl if it's numb. . . .) Try to keep the students focused on the problem at hand, steering discussion back to the reading when necessary.

Again, summarize. As in lectures, be sure to use the blackboard frequently to summarize the points raised. This is particularly important for class discussions that seem to take on a life of their own. Sometimes you'll need to corral the discussion by organizing it into relevant points. Some instructors love to sit back and watch a class move from one discussion to another, sometimes to the point of contention among the students. A little controversy is healthy for the class, but you don't want it spinning out of control. As an instructor, it's your job to try to keep the students close to the topic.

INTERNATIONAL STUDENT TA'S

International students may face special challenges in the classroom. Some TA's may encounter language or cultural barriers with their students. If your English is heavily accented, you can still get your message across in a number of ways. Handouts covering assignments, instructions, and important dates will keep students from having any misunderstandings about the course requirements. You can use discussion sections more

GETTING YOUR CLASS TO TALK

Beginning discussions may be difficult at first. The first few days of class you should call on students to get them used to participating. After a while, as students do more of the reading, it will be easier for them to contribute their analyses of a topic without the fear that they will be "wrong."

Here, only the research you produce is considered heavily in your departmental evaluations. Having students who like you won't get you far if you spend less time on research.

—Dale, Ph.D. student,

Psychology

frequently and draw on audiovisual aids to supplement your lectures. The Berkeley TA handbook recommends that international grad student TA's audit an undergraduate course before they begin teaching to get accustomed to the cultural differences in the classroom.

IS THERE A TEACHER IN THIS CLASS?

You've spent all night in the lab troubleshooting a botched experiment. You've got to teach a class at 8:30 a.m and you're completely unprepared. Occasionally being unprepared for a class is unavoidable—an unforeseen problem arises in your research, your child is sick at home with the flu, or your adviser just informed you that he or she is leaving town for six weeks and you need to get together now to go over chapters of your dissertation.

There are a few strategies you can adopt to keep from admitting to your students that you're unprepared to teach. Leading the class into a discussion will keep you from having to lecture on the material. You can start out by posing a problem related to the last assignment and then breaking the class up into smaller discussion groups. Or ask one side of the class to come up with questions about the reading and let the opposite side answer them. Another approach is to ask students to review the reading and come up with a question they want answered. Ask students to write down their questions, collect them, and review them. You can answer a couple of questions, then turn the rest over to the students for their input. Also, if you have time to arrange it in advance, use a film or video and ask students to relate it to the reading.

WILL THIS BE ON THE TEST?

My recommendation is that you test students early on in the term to get an idea of their progress. If they know a test is coming up quickly, they'll pay closer attention to the material and get the reading done on time. If the course involves a lot of reading, you may want to give daily quizzes to make sure they keep up. Both the first test and the quizzes should be minimally counted toward the final grade; they are more diagnostic tools for you than barometers of the students' abilities. Your students should know the grading criteria for each test. If you were not specific on the syllabus, explain how exams will be graded in detail. You may even want to pass out a handout with guidelines for the test, topics to be covered, and format.

Departmental standards may decide the format and content of your exams. So much the better; you'll know the approach and have sample tests given in the past to use. If you're designing exams on your own, show them to other TA's or professors before you give them. Take the exams yourself and have models of the "perfect" test to use for grading. This is particularly important for essay tests, where grading is more subjective and students have more room to complain. You want students to know that you are fair and objective in your grading policies. If students come to you with grievances, show them your model test and offer suggestions for improving their test-taking skills on the next exam.

GRADING THE INSTRUCTOR

Some schools only provide students with evaluation forms for the professor teaching a course, not the TA's. You will be evaluated, however, by the professor in charge of a course if you assist him or her in the classroom. Evaluation forms with concrete student comments give the supervising professor a much better idea of your expertise in the classroom. Their comments also provide insights on improving your classroom teaching style.

TA UNIONS

Lately the role of teaching assistants in the university administration has become controversial. Budget con-

FORM A TA GROUP

If your department does not have a TA group that meets even informally to share experiences and trade information, get one started. A regularly scheduled TA meeting to discuss grading, teaching tips, test design, and so on will help you enormously in acquiring a comfort level in the classroom.

The group also acts as a supportive network during stressful times when you're trying to balance teaching with other responsibilities. If, after discussion with other TA's, you all see problems with the workload or compensation you receive, work as a group with the department to resolve difficulties.

straints in universities have forced many schools to increase the TA's workload. These overworked grad students are beginning to actively voice their discontent. TA's have gone on strike or formed unions to negotiate for higher wages, lighter teaching loads, and/or additional benefits. According to one student, a strike at the University of Virginia in the 1980s by English TA's forced undergraduate English classes to a screeching halt. As a result, the TA's received a lighter teaching load and higher support level. Large campuses like Berkeley and NYU have TA unions already in place. Some professors consider teaching requirements as paying your dues to get a degree. But if TA's are commonly devoting 35-40 hours per week just on classroom work alone, there's a definite problem. Overloading TA's with teaching burdens only increases the time to degree, reflecting badly on the whole department's reputation.

Lobbying through the graduate student association may be the best method of negotiating better benefits. It's always preferable to work within the system, and without hostility to resolve any points of disagreement. Don't jump first to organizing a strike without first going through the channels available to address problems. Request more grad student participation on faculty committees. Try to get involved in the administrative functions of the department so that TA's have more visibility and input in policy decisions. Sometimes faculty are so busy they're just not aware of TA grievances. Make them aware.

If the teaching policies are university-wide, go through the student government organization, which exists for just such a purpose. Striking and forming unions should be grad students' last resort, after they have exhausted all other university resourses.

RESEARCH (OR, THE DAILY GRIND)

CHAPTER 7

Selections from "A Day in the Life of a Grad Student" (Part 1)

6:30   *Wake up and lie awake in bed.*

6:31   *Realize you spent $18 on last night's dinner. Means no eating out for the next six weeks.*

6:32   *Hit snooze button. Go back to sleep.*

7:00   *Wake up suddenly with heart in mouth when you realize you didn't hit the snooze button—you turned it off.*

7:01   *Fall asleep again.*

7:44   *Wake up with heart in mouth again.*

7:45   *Ready to go to school. Will shave tomorrow. Will eat early lunch at (Denny's/Penny's/Lenny's/Dinko's/whatever cafeteria). . .*

Source: http://www.cs.umbc.edu/www/graduate/aday.html

You are now entering the phase of grad school that is the least structured. At this point you're out of classes, finished with exams, and moving into Daily Life: research. Whether you knew it or not when you started,

DON'T WAIT TO SET UP YOUR OFFICE

You're setting up an office just as you would in a corporate or industry job. This is the first step in moving from student to professional, and it's important that you organize your work space early. It will save you time later when the thesis/dissertation research starts to pile up.

conducting research is the defining feature of your graduate career. If you plan to stay in academe, it will be the defining feature of your academic life.

ORGANIZATION IS VITAL

During the research phase of your graduate career you will have the least guidance from faculty and other students, so before you dive in, you'll need to set up a schedule for organizing your time and building a comfortable daily routine. Establishing a routine will help you get through those periods when you feel isolated and unmotivated—periods that can hurt the progress of your research. Even though you may be spending less time on campus, you still need to be visible both inside and outside the department. You should also begin forming valuable networks to enhance both your research goals and future career opportunities. And finally, this chapter includes guidelines for developing effective research techniques and preparing grant proposals.

FINDING YOUR SPACE

Whether it's your TA office, library carrel, or your home, you need a central location for work. Sometimes you'll be juggling all three work spaces, and it'll be easy for articles, books, notes, and calendars to be spread out over miles. Designate a space for thinking and writing, for filing papers, lab reports, and articles, for storing and categorizing books, and for keeping your calendar. Most importantly, designate nonwork spaces, particularly if you'll be doing most of your work at home. If you watch TV to relax, don't use the TV room as a storage space for books and files if you can avoid it. You'll end up staring at the work more than the TV.

SCHEDULING YOUR TIME

This section could also be called "Stress Management." Without the structure of classes or the landmarks of exams, you may begin to feel like you're navigating without a compass. Although you're teaching and/or working in the lab, you are also now responsible for doing research on your own. Some students find this independence to be liberating. Others miss the constant positive reinforcement from grades, other students, and faculty. At this point in the program you know you're supposed to be reading up on your field and narrowing your area of specialization. But now that you're out of classes, you're not exactly sure how best to organize your daily life to coordinate independent research.

The key to setting up a comfortable routine is to know your limitations. If you know you never do work on Friday nights, don't schedule that time for lab work or reading—make Friday nights your playtime. Plan your work in advance, but do it in concise, manageable stages. When I'm juggling several projects, I map out my schedule a month in advance.

Below are some items to include in your daily routine to preserve your mental health.

Exercise. You probably have more free time on your hands than you did when you were taking classes. This doesn't mean that you have less work to do. On the contrary, most likely your workload will increase, and with more work you will experience more stress. Grad students joke that "at least you get to choose *which* 20 hours you work each day."

It may seem during this time that exercise is the last thing you have time for. But if you haven't been getting any regular exercise up to this point, you need it now. A regular exercise schedule will help you gain the discipline you need to do other activities independently. And three days a week of swimming, cycling, or pumping weights at the gym does more than just make you look great. It also clears your head.

Exercise also puts problems in perspective—away from your lab or office, the pressures of your work seem manageable. At times you need to get out of the house and back into the world. Don't underestimate the value

ROME WASN'T BUILT IN A DAY

The only way to get a big project done is to break it down. Let this become your mantra while you're doing independent research. If you're constantly thinking of the Big Picture, the amount of work to be done will terrify you into complete paralysis.

EUREKA!

Many times students have some of their best ideas while they're running laps around the track. Exercise can be a magical catalyst for problem solving, as effective as a good night's sleep to yield sudden insights and inspiration.

of 30 minutes of aerobic activity. A healthier body means a sharper brain and a more relaxed psyche.

Social life. Most grad students have forgotten what it is to have a life outside their research: "Social life? What's that?" With a more demanding work schedule, it's very easy to let your social life fade into oblivion. But you shouldn't neglect your friends, particularly those outside grad school.

Like exercise, maintaining outside friendships can be invaluable for giving you a much-needed break from your research. When you're setting up your daily routine, schedule a couple of evenings a week just for fun. Find out what's going on in the city and on campus and take advantage of the opportunities for new experiences and new people. Sometimes an unrelated activity can actually contribute to your research—helping you to see a problem in a new way, giving you new ideas, even changing the focus of your research. Join organizations devoted to your interests.

Family. An entire book could be written on balancing family life with graduate school. This balancing act can be extremely complicated, especially for women who serve as the caretaker for their families. Your family can be a wonderful source of support while you're at home working on independent research. As grad school becomes more demanding, however, it will be tempting to give family members less of your attention.

In addition, traditional household responsibilities may shift when one partner is in grad school, adding potential stress to the relationship. A woman in grad school may have less time for household management tasks like shopping and cooking, and a father in grad school may end up with more child-care duties if his partner works full-time away from home. When one partner is in grad school, the rule is that there are no rules! The best advice my husband and I ever received in managing responsibilities is not to compare ourselves to couples in traditional roles. Find the system that works for *your* household.

Make sure everyone knows your schedule. With household duties changing, it's imperative that your daily routine be clearly understood by the whole family. Children in particular need a consistent routine of "work" and "play." Your kids and your partner should know when you will be working and when you will be available for them. Your family may have trouble at first realizing the difference between working at home and relaxing at home. This is the biggest difficulty when your home is also your office.

Your partner is not your colleague. Some partners enjoy hearing the detailed and technical aspects of graduate work. In fact, many help edit and type papers and give their partners a sounding board for ideas. By listening, your partner feels involved, and he or she shares in your successes. But you shouldn't take advantage of a supportive partner. Even the most understanding partner may get tired of hearing about an area of interest he or she doesn't share. Your partner should not become a substitute for other students in the department—he or she is not getting the degree. Maintaining your friendships with other grad students for information, idea sharing, and support will keep your work life and home life properly balanced.

Communicate when problems arise. Some students say that their partners have been very unsupportive, even to the point of trying to sabotage their careers. It's one thing for your partner not to share the same enthusiasm for your research, but it's quite another thing for your partner to feel threatened by your work. If you sense a problem, direct and immediate communication may help you find the source of resentment. It may be that you have been so absorbed in your research that your partner feels neglected. Because of the major changes in daily responsibilities, some partners have more trouble than others making the adjustment. Sympathy, rather than defensiveness, is the best way to get the kind of support you need.

That said, you must also be prepared to stand your ground if you feel your partner is making impossible demands on your time. Explain your daily workload so your partner has a sense of your responsibilities.

Try to help your partner see that grad school is *not* a hobby, but a full-time job, sometimes requiring more than 40 hours per week of your time.

Dealing with doting parents. Younger, single students may have family challenges of another kind—from their

KEEP YOUR WORD

If you've promised to do something with your partner or your family, don't cancel out, no matter what kind of pressing work you may have. If you let them down, you cannot count on them to be understanding and supportive. You want them to be with you after grad school is over. Remember your longer-term goals of emotional health and happiness.

PROUD PARENTS

In general, parents will come to respect your time once they recognize how important grad school is to you. And, as they come to understand the demands of your work, they will also come to appreciate and share in your success. Soon enough they will be telling their friends about your first conference or publication!

parents. Unless they have been to grad school themselves, parents typically have trouble understanding the demands of a grad school workload, and they may continue to treat your schedule like they did when you were in college. It's ironic but true that you have to set boundaries with parents as much as you would with children, and you have to stick to your limits. Sometimes you may not even be able to come home for holidays. Parents are good at manipulation—they've had years of practice on you. But if the work has to come first, stand your ground. This can be one of the best (but hardest) maturing experiences for young grad students, as they learn to put their needs above their parents' desires.

Research assistant. You'll also be including some form of work in your schedule—usually as an RA or TA. It's important to keep your employment schedule consistent, and for science students to work out with faculty in advance when they will be scheduled for lab time. Faculty advisers may ask you to work so many hours in the lab that your other projects fall behind. Don't let the lab time cut into your independent research and reading, unless the work will directly contribute to your CV or thesis/dissertation. Remember that it's a boss's job to get as much work out of you as possible for the least amount of money.

Teaching. Another juggling act is combining teaching with research and your personal life (see Chapter 6). Remember: you can spend 40 hours per week on your class, or you can spend 10. The grad students that spend extra time preparing for their classes do it because they love teaching in general, because it offers them more or different rewards than their research. These instructors are a boon to the profession. Too few grad students greet their teaching responsibilities with enthusiasm. But despite your zest for teaching, keep in mind that you must develop a *range* of skills for success in grad school, and don't let valuable research time slip away. The ultimate goal is to get out of school so you can start getting paid real wages for your expertise in the classroom.

Outside job. I know plenty of students who work full-time in nonacademic jobs, go to grad school full- or part-time, and have families. I am frankly in awe of them.

There are almost no strategies on time management I could offer to these courageous folks that they are not already employing by necessity. My only suggestion here is the same as that for RA's in the lab working with faculty employers. If getting the degree is your highest priority, and work is only a way to pay the bills, make sure you don't let your employer take advantage of you. Learn to say "no." Your employer should understand that your degree is an important goal to you, and there are times when it has to come first. Usually employers respect continuing education—many have advanced degrees themselves—and will help you with scheduling the occasional conflicts between work and school deadlines. Many companies even offer financial support for student-employees.

Research. I'll go over research techniques later in this chapter, but here I want to stress scheduling time specifically for research. Because you will do much of this work independent of the lab or the classroom, it's easy to let this time dwindle when other responsibilities seem more pressing.

The best advice I can offer here (and I've used it myself in writing this book) is to have a specific idea of what you want to *accomplish* during research time. Don't say to yourself, "I'll read 4 hours Tuesday night and write 4 hours Wednesday night." Say instead, "I'll read four articles Tuesday night and I'll write five pages Wednesday night." You need a clear goal for the time you've set aside.

NETWORKING

Networking is the cornerstone of good research. Even the most competent students can't access all of the available resources on their own. By now you're getting interested in particular aspects of the field and should be looking for colleagues inside and outside the department interested in the same specialty. Making contacts not only helps you find additional resources, but also gives you the opportunity to publicize your work. That equals more career opportunities in the future.

CAMPUS JOB?

If you aren't getting the support you need in your current job, you can usually find another job where you will. Consider getting a job on campus. University employers are accustomed to having employees who are working on degrees and will cut you a surprising amount of slack.

A SCHEDULING CAVEAT

Never say, "I'll work on my research paper all weekend." Remember saying this to yourself in college, when it meant, "Maybe it'll get done and maybe it won't." If you schedule your time this way, you'll begin working on your research paper at midnight on Sunday. Remember, too, that your brain will just quit on you after about 4 hours. Don't overestimate the capacity of your gray matter when you're organizing your schedule.

MEMBERSHIP IN PROFESSIONAL ORGANIZATIONS

Joining academic organizations in your field should be a priority at this stage. Usually for as little as 10 or 20 dollars a year you can become a student member of an organization in your field. You will hear about upcoming conferences, publications, grant opportunities, and on-line resources. You don't need to join every organization out there—just find the biggest and/or the best. Down the road, as your interests become more specialized, you may find a smaller organization that's perfectly suited to your research interests.

JOB NETWORKING

Another benefit of meeting people in on-line groups is finding out details about hiring at universities or other institutions. If a tenure-track position at a university gets posted and you're interested in hearing more about the department, you can use the Internet to find students in that department and get the low-down.

THREE KINDS OF NETWORKS

When you begin forming relationships with your colleagues, you're looking for three things: information, career opportunities, and support.

Information exchange. Access to information contributes most directly to your research. The easiest way to make contacts with experts in your area is to join an Internet newsgroup devoted to your topic of interest. These Internet groups are easy to find by using Web search engines such as Yahoo, Web Crawler, Lycos, InfoSeek, and others. If you're not yet comfortable with the Web, professors and other students may be able to recommend some of the best and largest newsgroups. They can help you join or point you to others who can get you into these on-line discussion groups. It's much easier to contact one of the big guns in the field if you've read his or her posts on the group list. Even though you don't know them personally, you'll know how to approach them after seeing how they interact with the group (helpful, contentious, reticent, etc.).

Career opportunities. The Internet is your best friend here, too. Most of the Calls for Papers (CFPs) are published on-line. And scholars looking for contributors to an anthology will post to related newsgroups rather than paying to advertise in an academic publication. In general, you'll find out about publishing opportunities much faster on the Net. Many collaborative projects (and partnerships) begin on e-mail even before you start meeting people at conferences.

In all fields, but especially in the sciences, journal articles are published a long time after the research has been completed. Published research becomes outdated very quickly, so you can't stay on top of hot topics simply by reading journals in the library. You have to get involved in on-line networks to hear about—and contribute to—work in progress. Many times you will make contacts through on-line discussion groups and begin corresponding privately about detailed aspects of your work. It's not uncommon for a fellow student to ask you to read over a paper before it has been submitted to a journal. Nor should you be shy about asking others to review your work, both faculty and students.

Support. This networking comes predominantly from other grad students. Some of my closest friends, those who offer the most encouragement and support, are people I've never even met before. I have long-standing e-mail friendships with students all over the country, and we have offered each other much-needed "Kudos!" and pats on the back. Developing friendships over e-mail is quite common, and fellow grad students can be a valuable resource for idea and information sharing as well as emotional encouragement. I feel less trepidation bouncing an idea off one of my grad student friends before I approach a faculty member in my own department. And everyone I know feels the same.

Remember, too, that grad students will be your future colleagues. Down the road a bit, you may be involved in collaborative research projects with the same people you met on e-mail.

LEARNING TO WORK AND PLAY WELL WITH OTHERS

Strong e-mail networks, however, should not be a substitute for networks within your department. They should complement each other. As you spend more time working at home, don't lose touch with those friends you made in classes. Try to get together regularly for socializing, even though scheduling the time will be more difficult as your work gets more involved. You'll need these friends now more than ever.

Also, stay connected to department activities. The quickest way to get paranoid about your future is to lose touch with the department goings-on. Visibility is two-fold—you see them and they see you. If you have an office on campus, try to get the bulk of your work done there, just to be close to other grad students and professors. Don't skip guest lectures and special seminars because you don't think you have time. For science students, it's important to stay involved in regular research meetings if the department offers them. Some departments also have regularly scheduled meetings for students to read their research papers from recent conference presentations. Find out what the other students are working on.

Social problem solving. Problem solving of the academic kind is a snap for you—problems of the "people" kind, however, make you tremble in fear. Dealing with conflicts is another one of those survival skills that no one will teach you, but one that invariably separates the average student from the rising star. The impression you make inside the department is crucial. It's important now, after exams are over, to become more like a colleague than a student. As you become more independent, you want to look active, enthusiastic, and mature. Profs should be treated as coworkers in the office, not parents guiding you through your program.

Avoid gossip. Remember that the information grapevine is also a gossip grapevine. You want to get all of the gossip you can, of course, but you don't want to be the subject of it! In your interactions with other students and professors, keep your personal life to yourself. You may find one grad student (and only one, usually) with whom you can safely confide every sordid detail of your life, every mistake you've made in school, every doubt and frustration you've had about joining the profession. Under no circumstances should you share this kind of personal information with faculty members. Even your family life should be kept out of this academic "office." You have to present an image of relative contentment and confidence, no matter what doubts you may have. You can listen to the gossip, but try not to say anything negative about what you hear.

Remember what mom taught you! "If you can't say anything nice, don't say anything at all."

Work it out yourself. If you have a problem with another student or faculty member, work it out with the person involved if at all possible. Grad students who have gone over a professor's head to resolve personality conflicts have always ended up regretting it. Complaining almost always hurts the grad student and not the professor involved in the conflict. This is also true when a problem arises between two grad students. Not only does it demonstrate a lack of maturity (it looks like you're running to the principal when someone calls you a bad name), but other professors may consider you a troublemaker. They may be less willing to help you when you need them. Sometimes you have no recourse and may just have to suck it up and deal with a bad attitude from a professor, a bad grade, or bad working conditions. But if you're assertive in the beginning of your relationships with professors and students, and get inside info about department politics early in the game, you should be able to sidestep these personal conflicts altogether.

A Day in the Life of a Grad Student (Part 2)

8:03   *Arrive at school. Realize your officemate arrived earlier today; must have gotten more work done.*

8:04   *Pass by adviser's office; chat with secretary to find out if he is coming in today. He is, darn. Need to start work on the draft due this afternoon.*

8:15   *Read e-mail.*

9:00   *For jump start: go to soda machine.*

9:05   *Kick soda machine; promise yourself to call up the company and ask for your money back. Wonder why they would believe you.*

9:33   *Start printing out loads of stuff that may be vaguely related to your work.*

9:41   *Early morning stupefaction.*

10:59   *Drop in at adviser's office and borrow something you don't need to remind him you're working hard on your project.*

11:45   *Print out some slides for afternoon's draft of presentation.*

11:47   *Print them again, you forgot to change the date from last presentation.*

Research is a continually evolving process. After only a year it's impossible to be pinned down to a particular topic, so you just have to feel your way along. By working on different papers, you'll begin to see a common thread running through them. The more work you do, the more cohesive a research idea becomes.
—Colin, Ph.D. student, Computer Science

11:49 *Print another copy in case this one gets lost.*

11:51 *Completely forget about suing the soda machine company.*

RESEARCH TECHNIQUES

This section does not tell you how to use the library or conduct your experiments. What it does cover are ways you can make the most of your research time, along with some of the most common time wasters.

What are the best resources for beginning research in your area of interest? Before you head for the library's on-line catalog, ask around the department. Grad students in your field who've been around longer know the general publications you'll need to review before you get started. Your professors will make recommendations, and you can look at reading lists from past exams and from other students. Many times students will let you copy their articles and borrow their books, saving you library time and copying fees. These sources will be a solid first step in beginning research.

RESEARCH TIME-SAVERS

Here are strategies for making the most of your research time.

- Keeping a research notebook
- Effective library searching
- Saving key words
- Dividing work into stages
- Speed-reading
- Annotating your sources
- Archiving files
- Finding a research buddy

Keeping a research notebook. Science students have probably already received this advice from their professors. For them, a research notebook contains dated material on experiments, including the purpose of the experiment; information on lab equipment used; data collected; calculations; lab procedures; results; and ideas for modified or future experiments. But a research notebook can be a valuable tool for students in the sciences *and* the arts.

Your notebook should also be used for jotting down flashes of inspiration. In reading over a long period of time, you will begin to see connections between ideas, intersections of topics in widely diverse publications. The notes you take may be the germ of an independent research idea. Write down the connections you make during your reading, and cite the sources that inspired them. Later you will see that you've been building an idea for independent research out of your reading. And remember to *read* your notebook from time to time.

Effective library searching. You don't want to reinvent the wheel. Do a literature search at the library to be sure that your brilliant idea is "original" and "significant." The quickest library shortcut is to look at a review article on all the literature published in your research area during the past year. All disciplines have (at least) one annual publication like this—basically an annotated bibliography of everything that's been published in the field. This is "one-stop shopping." Someone else has already gone to the trouble to read the publications and evaluate their quality. You've got the easy job—writing down references of well-reviewed articles and books related to your area of interest.

This search does not need to be exhaustive, at least not in the beginning. Later you may want to go backward in time, but at the start keep your search limited by date and close to the present. Get an idea of the ongoing scholarly discussion of your topic and the current or speculated direction of the research. Knowing the scholarly "conversation" will tell you almost everything you need to begin developing your own ideas.

Key word saving. It's important to locate and record references. It's equally important to note how you found your sources. If you're using the library's on-line catalog, write down the key words used in your search. The

A GOOD RESEARCH NOTEBOOK INCLUDES:

- References of landmark books and articles
- Citations of texts to look up later
- Names of faculty you come across often in your research
- Upcoming conferences of interest
- Ideas for future conference papers or publications
- Funding opportunities

"BACKDOOR" SEARCHING

Computer indexing varies tremendously from program to program. If one set of key words doesn't get you exactly where you want to go, try more—try everything! Take an article you've already located and look it up. Once you get it on the screen, see how it's indexed. Then you can use those key words in your search to find related literature. This is a handy backdoor strategy for finding key words when you're using a new or confusing search system.

same goes for using *Dissertation Abstracts* or on-line periodical searches. If you only look up three articles out of the six you found in a search, you may want to look at the other three articles down the road. Then you will need to know how you found the six articles in the first place.

Dividing your work into stages. After a successful trip to the library, you may come home with 10 books and 20 articles on your topic. Now you've got to read them! The stack itself is intimidating, and just looking at it can overwhelm even the most diligent student. Remember your grad school mantra: break it down. Schedule the reading in stages, including time for transferring notes and references to your computer. Sometimes I even separate my books into stacks for each day so the reading looks more manageable. Learning to do this now will contribute to a shorter time to degree when you start working on your thesis/ dissertation in earnest. Know what you want to accomplish in your reading and have a clear path to get there.

When you're scheduling your work, it can be very tempting to do the no-brainer work first and then move on to the creative or analytical parts. I like to check my e-mail before I get started on my work, but I limit my time on the Internet to 1 hour, regardless of how much mail I've got coming in. Don't wait too long to do your thinking. It's much easier to think when you first sit down to work and then do administrative work after a few hours. Reward yourself with grunt work after you've done the difficult writing or thinking.

Speed-reading. If you're reading every word of an article or book, you're wasting valuable time and falling behind the progress of other students. No one reads everything. It's important when you're conducting research to have some idea of what you're looking for before you find it. If you're researching a topic in the library and find references from several journals, start out with the articles from leading journals. And don't race to the copying machine with articles in hand. Before you spend your money, take a few minutes to review the articles.

First read the abstract or the intro paragraphs to see how an idea is presented. Does it cover what you're looking for? Many times the title will be misleading. Is the article well written? By reading the last paragraph you can see if the main idea holds together. And, most important of all, check the bibliography. You'll begin to see that certain articles and books are cited over and over again. In cases where you're pressed for time, look at the bibliography first.

Annotating your sources. As you read through articles and books, make notes on how useful each source was. Type up all of the sources you've read and include an informal "review" of the article or book. Write down whether a source was helpful or useless, what chapters or pages were relevant, and what publications you might want to look at again at a later stage. If you don't annotate your sources, you'll end up rereading them (and kicking yourself when you realize it).

Archiving files. If you're a student in computer science, you already know how important it is to archive files. Keeping track of your files saves time so you don't repeat your work. Create subdirectories for different projects or aspects of a single research project, and periodically clean out your files. Keep a hard copy of the most important documents in your computer and file them in clearly labeled file folders. Save outdated but valuable work such as class papers, older lab reports, and conference papers onto floppy disks. Label the disks and print out a file list for each one. You may want to add annotations to the files in case the file names seem cryptic to you later.

Finding a research buddy. Losing your motivation? Remote control for the TV leaping into your hands seemingly of its own free will? You need a research buddy. Your research buddy doesn't have to be in your specific area, or even at the same school. My research buddy lives close by but attends another university, and we get together informally just to talk about our ideas and research. Though you can make friends on-line, your buddy should be someone you can get together with face-to-face. Your buddy will read over your papers, encourage your ideas, sometimes even collaborate with you on projects. He or she should not be in direct competition with you. If necessary, schedule regular times and places to meet so you don't lose touch with

SPEED-READING WITH BOOKS

Learn to cruise through books in search of the heart of the matter. A good introduction gives an overview of the author's argument. From there, you can use the index to find pages that cover material related to your research topic. The book's conclusion may also offer some good ideas. Many times an author will include possibilities for future research, ideas you may want to take up on your own.

ON-LINE ARCHIVING

Find a method for tracking your on-line research. You can use your research notebook to keep track of helpful URLs, on-line journals, and academic pages with links to research in different areas of your field. Whatever method you choose, be consistent. And take notes in one reliable place.

Don't fool yourself into thinking that e-mail messages to fellow grad students constitute actual work. Get the real work done first. Then you can brag about it to your e-pals.

one another during stressful work periods. You'll need your buddy most when you have the heaviest workload. He or she can keep you sharp, motivated, involved, and on your academic toes.

RESEARCH TIME WASTERS

Three of the biggest time wasters are of the electronic variety . . .

- E-mail
- Computer games
- Phone/TV
- Overscheduling yourself
- Underestimating the time to accomplish tasks

E-mail. Technically, you're doing research, right? Right now the perfect citation or grant opportunity is sitting out there waiting for you in cyberspace. Networking on e-mail, as I said before, is one of the best options for research opportunities and information gathering.

Unfortunately, e-mail can also be the biggest time waster of a grad student's career. The first three months after I discovered the Net, I spent as much as 4 hours a day surfing, subscribing, fingering, gophering, and MOOing. I realized, almost too late, that my work was falling behind even as I was making friends all over the globe. It had to stop. I disciplined myself instead to do all of my research and daily work first, and to reward myself with the Net when I was done. It worked, and I've used this method ever since.

Computer games. I've read that some companies have systematically removed "Doom" from their networks because it brought worker productivity to a virtual halt; I know people who have deleted computer games from their home PCs because they couldn't get any work done. You will be spending much of your time in front of the computer screen, an open invitation to dial-up on your modem line or double click on Solitaire for a quick game. But if you're not really in the mood to work anyway, playing one computer game invariably leads to another. Computer games are exhausting if you play them for very long, and suddenly all of your creative energy is used up. My suggestion here is the same as my advice about the Net: use games as your reward for a job well *done*.

Phone/TV. I don't use the phone much anymore since I got on-line, but (unfortunately) not all of my friends and family have e-mail accounts! You will get calls when you're in the middle of thinking through a difficult problem. If you believe you can get back to your train of thought after talking to your friend about her latest boyfriend, you're wrong. By the time you get back to the problem, whatever flashes of inspiration you had will be gone. Especially when you're reading, it's tempting to answer the phone. You're not really doing anything—not writing, not thinking. But even a couple of hours a day of interruptions can affect your productivity. You need large chunks of time just for thinking. The TV is worse because you can watch it at your convenience. Only use TV for limited brain breaks. I have a few programs that I watch with regularity. Then I turn the set off and get back to work.

Overscheduling yourself. Can't say no? Too many opportunities— not enough time? With more recognition and achievement comes more opportunity, but like anything else, you have to prioritize your time. I got involved in founding our department's graduate student association, and with a few other students devoted almost a month's time exclusively to setting it up. While I don't regret the time I spent on this project—the results were very rewarding—I said "no" to related association projects later on.

Underestimating the time to accomplish tasks. This goes under the subheading of "Know Thyself." Don't make the common mistake of underestimating how long it will take to finish a project. Once you start missing your deadlines, it is easy to degenerate into indecision, procrastination, and eventual crisis. Try to give yourself good lead time for new projects. If you complete tasks before your scheduled deadlines, so much the better!

"NO" IS NOT A DIRTY WORD

It's easy for one project to take you over, especially when you're full of enthusiasm and good intentions. But your first duty is to yourself and your career. If you're offered an opportunity, be sure to weigh the time commitment against the career rewards. Usually a new project will only contribute one line to your CV—there's no place on the CV to show how many hours you put into a task. Professors respect the word "no" almost as much as they are delighted by the word "yes." Don't worry that turning down one opportunity means you won't get others down the road. You will.

GRANT PROPOSALS

You may have to prepare grant proposals as part of your graduate education. One of the most valuable skills you can have, whether you stay in academe or go into industry, is the ability to convince others that your ideas are worth funding. If you pursue an academic career, grant writing will take up a large portion of your time. Grants decide your academic future—tenure, post-docs, opportunities to publish and or travel, and better job offers.

If you're a first-time grant writer, you should keep a couple of things in mind. First, don't reach for the moon with your first proposal. The best way to get grants as a novice is to start small—find "little" grants, local granting agencies, or internal grants from your university. Granting agencies tend to award money to people who already have a track record of getting grants. Receiving a grant of $1,000 means that you'll most likely get more money from your next proposal. Start locally, start small, but start now!

FIRST STEP: YOUR UNIVERSITY AND DEPARTMENT

How do you find out about grant opportunities? Every university has a department called something like the "Research Office" or "Grants and Research Office." These are staffed by people devoted to poring over all the grant sources out there and finding opportunities suitable for their academic researchers. Most agencies that offer grants send universities either Requests for Applications (RFAs) or Requests for Proposals (RFPs). These include all the information you'll need, including amounts available, deadlines, and application guidelines. Usually the research office publishes a regular listing of grant opportunities. Many times the office will also list grants available for graduate study, including inside as well as outside funding opportunities. Find out if your university's research office has a computerized database that lists opportunities, award amounts, and guidelines.

The members of your department—faculty, staff, even other grad students—are great sources of information about grant sources and opportunities. Many faculty members are working with grant money on current projects, and they will be happy to let you see their proposals. Other grad students are receiving outside funding through individual grants and may be willing to share their experiences and expertise. The department staff may also keep a record of currently funded projects in the department and a list of grant opportunities. Your own department is a gold mine of information and resources, and poking around will save you valuable search time on your own.

FINDING GRANT SOURCES

You also want to be aware of publications and institutions that list grant opportunities in your field. Outside grants fall into two broad categories: government and foundation grants. You can find out about government grants by checking the *Catalog of Federal Domestic Assistance* (CFDA). This incredibly large and rather cryptic publication offers an overview of funding opportunities, including those for graduate education and fellowships.

For nongovernment grants, look at the latest copy of *Foundation Grants to Individuals* in the reference section of the library. Published by The Foundation Center, this guide includes financial data on foundations and companies that make grants—assets, expenditures, number, and amount of grants awarded—as well as information on grant programs and deadlines.

Many students consult the "Big Book of Grants," otherwise known as the *Directory of Research Grants*, published by Oryx Press. This directory is broken down into separate volumes by field. It is updated yearly, and the newest one will be on the reference shelf. Older editions can usually be checked out. I recommend that you take one of these home and keep it on your bookshelf for awhile.

The *Grants Register* publishes a list of funded grants from government and private sources at or above the graduate level. This is a great source for graduate students. It lists grant money available in the form of scholarships and fellowships, travel grants, competition prizes, and research grants.

If you think your research may be of interest to industry or corporate sponsors, take a look at Dorin

For any grant, the most helpful thing is to have an interested adviser. Failing that, it's good to have a few people to help you with ideas and read over the proposal for logic and grammar. It's important that specific aims be addressed as specific questions, and that the experimental method is one that has been shown—by you, if possible—to work. Preliminary results are probably one of the key indicators of grant acceptance.

—*Rami, Ph.D. student, Neuroscience*

Schumacher's *Get Funded!* published in 1992 by Sage Publications. Particularly for students whose research involves computers or electronic media, corporations may be willing to fund projects and/or donate equipment. Though they don't include a great deal of information on grants available to graduate students, other guides you might consult are the *Annual Register of Grant Support: A Directory of Funding Sources* and *The Foundation Directory*.

Organizations. Two well-known organizations keep up-to-date information on grant opportunities. The first is The Foundation Center, with offices all over the country. The Foundation Center, though geared in large part to offering services to organizations such as private foundations and universities, also offers seminars for individuals on grant proposals. Their offices maintain extensive libraries of information about foundations, including annual reports, grant guidelines, and lists of grant deadlines.

The other is The Grantsmanship Center in Los Angeles, California. This organization also sponsors seminars and training programs on grant writing. Like The Foundation Center, it is geared more toward organizations than individual academic research, but it publishes a newsletter called *The Grantsmanship News* that lists new opportunities and offers helpful tips on preparing proposals.

FINDING THE RIGHT TOPIC

You may think this heading should come before "Finding Grant Sources." Not so! Although you should have a general idea of the kind of research you want to carry out, knowing where the money is should influence your approach. Many times you will have to tailor your research idea to the guidelines and aims of a granting agency. Keep your mind open and your ideas flexible. You don't want to mislead a granting agency into thinking that you're interested in one approach or outcome, however, when in fact you intend to pursue another. That's the surest way to cut off any future funding. The grants network is small, and word will spread if you don't follow through on your projected proposal.

It's important to call a staff member at the granting agency to discuss your idea. Almost all granting agencies encourage you to discuss your idea before it goes in writing as a formal proposal. This is an important conversation—part networking, part interview. You need to sound mature, competent, and courteous. Have an outline of the components of your proposal in front of you and a set of questions you want to ask. But keep it brief. Try to get as much information as you can from faculty input before you pick up the phone.

DOING THE RESEARCH: THE LITERATURE REVIEW

For students who help their faculty advisers prepare grant proposals, the literature review will be the bulk of their responsibility. Faculty members may ask students to review the literature on a topic and write up their findings for the proposal itself. Students may also be asked to write up their research results from a pilot or preliminary study performed by the lab group. Helping out on these proposals while still a student is excellent training for learning the art of grantsmanship.

Here are some guidelines you should use, both in the initial research phase and in writing up your research for the proposal itself.

You're not recounting history. The literature review section of a proposal is a narrative explanation and justification of your research project. It does not need to be exhaustive. It should simply summarize the status of the ongoing discussion in this area: What are academics saying right now about this topic? What kinds of research are currently under way?

Once you've decided the topic's status, including results of recent studies and prospects for future

INPUT FROM PIs

Your best resource for molding your ideas to the expectations of a granting agency is to get in touch with PIs—*Principal* Investigators, not *private* investigators! PIs are usually senior faculty in the department, though they're sometimes postdocs, who have been granted funding in the past. They know how to play the funding game, and are usually willing to discuss your proposal with you. They may even be willing to read it over before you send it. If part of your qualifying exams includes preparing a grant proposal, you will automatically receive guidance from senior faculty.

research, you're done. You won't be able to show off your extensive reading of the subject area—the space provided for a literature review is brief, and rightly so. Remember that you're not writing an academic paper. The goal of the literature search is simply to convince the funding agency your project is hot and worthwhile.

Narrate, don't list. Remember, you're not writing a bibliography in this section of the proposal. Don't just list previous studies and articles on your subject. The research and studies you cite should justify your ideas precisely. You want to explain your reasons for conducting the study, not explain the topic as a whole. Try to keep in mind that you're telling the reviewers a story, a story with a lesson at the end: "Money should be spent to learn more about this issue."

Use research to point out gaps. Another strategy of the literature review is to show what it doesn't cover, as well as what it does. You may be able to justify your research project by showing where existing research is limited. A good literature review will reveal gaps in research, inadequate data collection techniques and/or errors of interpretation of existing data—suggesting not only that your idea is significant to the research community, but that your contribution will be original in the sense that it takes existing research a step further. By building off of other studies you show the reviewers that your project will contribute to the ongoing academic conversation.

Components of a grant proposal. When putting together the individual components of a proposal, remember the overall goal—persuasion. Each section of your proposal should be a sales pitch to the reviewers, demonstrating the project's significance and your competence for the job. Don't try to impress the reviewers using technical language—there's a difference between technical jargon and sophistication. If you want to impress the reviewers, do it with precision and clarity rather than obfuscation. The proposal should be comprehensible and interesting to any professional in the field.

The sections of a proposal may differ from agency to agency, but most request the following:

- **Cover letter (including title).** You should state, clearly and succinctly, the purpose of the project, its significance, and the anticipated results (for example, publication). The granting agency will index your proposal based on a key word in your title, so make sure your title is as specific as possible without being too long.
- **Project summary (abstract).** The abstract should run about 250 words and describe the project's short-term and long-term goals. It may also include a brief description of the methods used to carry out the project. Be sure to link your project's aims to the general goals of the granting agency.
- **Table of contents.** The published guideline will describe the format you should use to organize the table of contents.
- **Literature review.** The standard literature review for government grant proposals is 15 pages.
- **Experimental design and methods.** Here you will be describing any pilot studies you have conducted in the lab; subjects (human or animal) to be used; time line for proposed research; statistical methods and data collection techniques; data management and methods for interpretation of results.
- **Bibliography.** This administrative section includes citations of references listed in the literature review and abstract.
- **Biographical sketch or CV.** Your CV should be tailored specifically to match the particular project. This section will also include the credentials of other collaborators on the project such as research and lab assistants, statisticians, and administrative personnel.
- **Budget.** The budget will include costs associated with personnel—salaries, benefits, and consultant and contractor costs. Also included will be costs for overhead—space; equipment; consumables; travel; telephone; and copying, printing, and mailing. Do not underestimate your budget—ask for what you need, and estimate costs conservatively. It doesn't help to receive grant funding and then run out of money before the project is finished.

- **University facilities and equipment.** Reviewers will not only be evaluating you but also your affiliated university. You need to demonstrate in this section of the proposal that your university can supply the equipment and materials to support your research.
- **Supplementary documentation and/or appendices.** Particularly for projects that involve subject testing of humans or animals, supplementary documentation must be provided. Check the agency guidelines for what should be included. Don't burden reviewers with extraneous detail such as statistical charts, graphs, supplemental bibliographies, and the like, if they're not specifically requested.

WHY PROPOSALS ARE ACCEPTED

Keep these in mind when you are drafting the proposal:

1. The proposal addresses a problem significant to the research community and/or within the general public.
2. The applicant uses an innovative and insightful approach to the problem.
3. The applicant has a reasonable plan for implementation of the project.
4. The applicant is qualified to undertake the project.
5. The proposal not only relates to the agency's goals but also provides an immediate and direct benefit to the granting agency.
6. The anticipated results justify the budget.
7. The project can be successfully completed in the proposed time frame.

WHY PROPOSALS ARE REJECTED

1. The instructions are not followed (for example, deadlines not met, proposal outside agency guidelines, time line inadequate).
2. Presentation is sloppy.
3. The problem is either not significant or of such magnitude that the money requested will not adequately address it.
4. The text of the proposal is not integrated well with individual components.
5. The applicant justifies the problem in overly emotional or political terms.
6. The procedures are confused with the project's goals.
7. The agency approves of the project but does not believe the applicant is qualified.
8. The budget is unrealistic.
9. The granting agency knows that the idea has already been unsuccessfully attempted.
10. The agency does not have enough information to make a decision.

PRESENTATION COUNTS

A good proposal is a self-contained piece: like a publication, one chapter leads naturally to the next. Each component of the proposal should support the others. Think of the proposal as an architectural structure or a work of art. Design and content are intricately related—the overall presentation counts as much as information. Make sure the application is neatly typed and easy to read.

IF YOU'RE ACCEPTED

Before you celebrate your success—and you should—there are still a few questions left to ask the granting agency about your project. Mary Rubin, author of *How to Get Money for Research*, recommends talking with the granting agency to make sure the following information is clearly understood by both you and the granting agency:

1. Can you receive money from other granting agencies?
2. Must you devote yourself to the project full-time? If so, for how long?
3. What are the granting agency's overall responsibilities?

4. What final product obligations do you have to the granting agency—i.e., does the granting agency have the right of first refusal for publication of a funded manuscript?

IF YOU'RE REJECTED

Most agencies have a built-in feedback system as part of the review process. If your proposal is rejected—and this is not uncommon for the first-time grant writer—you will probably receive a report that outlines the proposal's weaknesses. At the very least it will explain why your proposal was rejected. Many times the reviewers will indicate if the proposal would be acceptable in another form, or if money might be available from the agency at a later date to fund the project in the same form.

If the granting agency doesn't provide feedback, it's perfectly acceptable for you to call the agency to talk about the reasons for the proposal's rejection. You should ask if the proposal can be resubmitted once it has been revised according to the agency's guidelines. You can also ask if the agency could recommend another organization that might be willing to support your project.

Don't be upset by a rejection. The competition is fierce, and good proposals do not always get funding. And be determined. Try again at a later date with the same agency, and expand your research to locate other agencies that might be more suitable to your project.

YOUR THESIS/ DISSERTATION

CHAPTER 8

A Day in the Life of a Grad Student (Part 3)

12:20	*Big Mac/Fries time. Drink a not-so-cold generic can of cola from your desk.*
1:00	*Group meeting with adviser.*
1:14	*Sudden awareness of one's shallowness. Resentment toward officemate for sucking up to your adviser. Reminded by your adviser that you need to do some more work for your literature survey.*
1:51	*Adviser hands you the reddened copy of your draft for corrections.*
1:51:02	*The 49-second urge to murder adviser begins*
1:51:52	*Realize that he or she controls your assistantship/grade/graduation possibility/graduation date/all job opportunities/the rest of your life.*
1:52:53	*Thank him or her.*
1:52:54	*Thank yourself for not saying something stupid.*

Your thesis/dissertation is the last big hurdle before graduation. Perhaps the best metaphor for completing a thesis or dissertation is not a hurdle, or even a hoop, but a long-distance marathon. Many students argue that working on a thesis/dissertation is less a test of their

Thesis/dissertation chapters are usually self-contained units. Most students are encouraged to write the chapters as self-standing documents so that they might be published more easily as articles in professional journals, sometimes even before the full thesis or dissertation is completed.

intellectual abilities than of their endurance and sheer willpower. For those doctoral students who drop out of a graduate program, this is almost always when it happens. Sometimes, funding may dry up in the fourth or fifth years of dissertation writing. But most students fail to get past the dissertation stage because of psychological factors—they burn out on their topic, they feel isolated from their families and/or the university community, or, as they get older, begin reevaluating the Ph.D. as a career goal.

Students will never say that a thesis/dissertation is a walk in the park. But it doesn't have to be a nightmare, either. This chapter offers advice on getting through both the structural and emotional challenges of finishing a thesis or dissertation. Because the "All But Dissertation" phenomenon is so common, several books are available on organizing and writing a thesis/dissertation, as well as dealing with the various psychological stresses of such a long-term independent project. Here I offer some of the best strategies and include suggestions from students who have made it through the long haul.

WHAT IS A THESIS/ DISSERTATION?

The content and organization of theses and dissertations vary in the sciences and humanities, but, in general, a master's thesis is a short research paper, approximately 50 pages or less. Students can usually complete a thesis in three to six months. Dissertations are written by students at the doctoral level. In the sciences, a typical Ph.D. dissertation may run only 100 pages. In the humanities, however, a 300-page dissertation is not uncommon. Because the average page length varies, the time it takes to complete a dissertation varies as well. Some science students spend as little as a year and a half or two years researching and writing a dissertation. In my own field, English, I know students who have spent four years or more on dissertation research and writing.

DO YOU REALLY NEED TO WRITE A THESIS?

Although traditionally a thesis has been required of all master's students, many fields now offer a non-thesis option for M.A./M.S. students. In lieu of doing a thesis, the department will usually require that you take additional classes. But you can take those classes in half the time it would take you to finish a thesis. It's no surprise, then, that a non-thesis option is very popular for students who do not plan on continuing for a doctoral degree. You should know that a thesis is of negligible importance to nonacademic employers. Most corporate and industry employers just want to know you have the degree and will evaluate you based on the reputation of the department/school and your grades.

In addition, it is becoming more common for students to forego a thesis even when they do plan to continue on to doctoral study. In general, schools do not weigh it heavily in your doctoral application, unless parts of it have been published.

I would suggest that if you have the option of graduating without a thesis, do so. By cutting out the thesis you will save yourself time and can move on to a doctoral program or a job that much sooner.

If you plan to go on to a doctoral degree and worry that schools will think you are less qualified or committed to research without the thesis, contact the graduate directors at prospective schools. Ask for their input on evaluating thesis vs. non-thesis applicants. Chances are they do not make a distinction between the two.

REMEMBER YOUR GOAL

You can use your thesis or dissertation as a starting point for later research on ground-breaking questions. Ultimately, however, the key to solving these fundamental issues is to get out of school and into the field where you will have the independence, funding, and credibility to pursue your ideas.

PICKING YOUR TOPIC

If you're committed to making it through the thesis/dissertation marathon, you should know something up front. It's possible that you are destined to change the world in some significant way. But frankly, academia does not encourage fundamental research at

WILL YOUR IDEA SHOW OFF YOUR TALENTS?

You want to select a project that fully demonstrates your intellectual abilities, your familiarity with methodology and theory, and your analytical skills. If you have developed unique talents or have a specialized background beyond those of your peers, find a topic that can highlight the full range of your experience and expertise.

the graduate level. In order to change the world you have to finish school, and that means following established guidelines and traditional formulas for completing your thesis/dissertation. Before you even begin thinking about a thesis/dissertation topic, selecting an adviser and committee members, and so on, you should recognize the limitations of conducting seminal research as a grad student.

Students just beginning to think about topics invariably jump straight to the biggest challenges in the field. Naturally, the overarching issues are the most intriguing. But as you begin doing research on some of these Grand Projects, you will usually find that some of the most prominent people in the field have already attempted, unsuccessfully, to resolve these fundamental questions. The trick is to narrow a big idea into a manageable project.

Consider the following questions:

1. Is your idea original? "Original" does not mean "seminal." You may end up replicating a pilot or preliminary study conducted by another university research group. While this may not seem like original research, your contribution in terms of gathering and analyzing data and drawing alternate or extended conclusions will be original.
2. Will your idea keep your interest? A lot of marriages don't last three or four years. Can you be wedded to this topic 'til degree do you part?
3. Do you have the experience and equipment needed? Your project must be manageable on several levels. You have to have the intellectual expertise to complete the project as well as access to and experience with the necessary physical resources. Are you comfortable with the equipment you need to complete the project? Do you know how to find, manage, and protect the rights of the subjects you want to use? Know your limits.
4. How much time and money will your project take? If your idea requires you to travel—visiting special libraries or labs at other universities—consider not only the cost but the time involved. Do you need outside people to help you set up your

project, such as statisticians, programmers, a typist, and so on? You'll need to factor in consultant costs.

5. Have you conducted any research on this topic or area before? If you're building a project from scratch, without having done any prior related research or lab work, you've got a lot of work to do. You don't know at this stage what factors are controllable and what kinds of problems might come out of nowhere. What data do you need? How will you collect and analyze it? And, equally important, how will you represent it? Will you have access to necessary resources both inside and outside the university? Are you sure you've thought of all the equipment and resources that may be needed? With so many uncertainties, it may be wise to stay with a topic where you have some expertise.

YOUR OWN IDEA VS. YOUR PROFESSOR'S

It's very common for students, particularly in the sciences, to select a topic based on the recommendation of a faculty member. Usually these students will find a research topic related to the ongoing work of their labs, expanding or refining one aspect of a large project supervised by a faculty member. There are pros and cons of developing your own idea vs. building off a professor's research interests. By choosing an independent project, you have more freedom and control in directing the progress of your dissertation. You also have more of an opportunity to learn a variety of research skills and techniques, rather than doing repetitive or unchallenging lab procedures (while the faculty member gets to do the "fun stuff"). The project is more likely to sustain your interest if you've designed it yourself.

There are good and bad features to working off of a prospective adviser's project. You can probably finish your dissertation more quickly and will have more

I was very fortunate in that my thesis provided the opportunity to publish early and frequently in my graduate career. My advice to beginning graduate students would be to choose a project that will allow you to publish before you graduate and that uses techniques that are in demand by employers. This could mean the difference between having several exciting employment and funding opportunities and working as a permanent postdoc.

—Patricia, Ph.D. graduate, Pharmacology

faculty guidance and assistance along the way. You will most likely not have to worry about funding. The faculty member who directs your project may have excellent contacts that can land you a good job; he or she may be working on a very prestigious research project that will help build your own reputation. Although the level of work may be less challenging than independently pursuing a project, it may also be easier, allowing you to devote more time to other worthwhile projects.

But working on one aspect of your professor's research, especially if the work you do is part of an outside grant project, involves serious considerations. You need to know from your professor what your responsibilities will be, including who gets credit for publishing your research. Make sure that funding will be available for the duration of your project, and find out how much time the project will take to complete. What happens if he or she leaves the university?

GENERATING IDEAS

If you've decided to develop your own idea for a topic, you can find great ideas from a variety of sources, not all of which are academic. Use the following sources to help point you to possible topics.

Copies of other theses/dissertations. To get a feel for the kinds of topics currently being pursued in graduate-level research, take a look at your department's recent theses and dissertations on file in the library. Not only will these give you an idea of the formal organization of a thesis/dissertation at your school, but they will also help you see the level of academic rigor expected in your own work. After looking through these, you should extend your search using *Dissertation Abstracts International*.

Academic journals. You will be reviewing the literature in the field as you narrow your general interests to a specific topic. Academic journals give you an idea of the kind of research being published, but remember: looking at journals alone won't tell you everything about hot topics in the field. You need to supplement journal research with networking and Internet resources (see Chapter 7).

Personal interests. Having a life outside the department does more than preserve your sanity; it also generates ideas for research. Keeping up with the news or watching a documentary on The Learning Channel can bring a flash of inspiration. So, too, can conversations with friends in different careers. You may find that your job, academic or nonacademic, also yields possible research questions.

A very common method of selecting a research topic is to weave together academic and personal interests. Parents may want to do research on children's education; female students may take up women's issues; international students may pursue research in cultural studies. Anything's up for grabs as a possible topic—computer games, animals, fashion, movies, jobs, politics, even sex! For those students who have a lot of freedom to choose their topics, they may find their interest levels are highest when they can explore issues near and dear to their hearts.

SELECTING AN ADVISER AND COMMITTEE

The most important decision you will make in your graduate career is selecting your thesis/dissertation adviser. Students do not exaggerate when they say that your adviser controls your life! The thesis/dissertation is not a totally independent endeavor. Although you may choose a topic on your own, conduct your own research, and write up the finished product, your adviser will shape and refine your project, suggesting revisions ranging from grammar and syntax to substantive alterations in your methodology or theory.

Many books recommend that you find an adviser who can serve as a mentor, i.e., a faculty member who takes a real interest in your success and acts as job facilitator, interested colleague, information source, and personal counselor. What the books don't say, however, is how

YOU'RE NOT ON *OPRAH*

Choosing a topic in which you have a vested interest is not an invitation to jump on a soapbox. Working on an intensely personal or politically charged issue may impair your objectivity, including the way you interpret data when it doesn't fit your hypothesis. You want to be enthusiastic about your topic, but you also want to be fair.

REMINDER ABOUT MENTORING

If you hadn't noticed already, faculty members are generally overworked, whether or not they are tenured. Being a true mentor involves a significant time investment with very little payoff. Even motivated and compassionate professors may be unable to "mentor" while completing their own projects.

rare these kinds of mentors are. Out of the hundreds of students I interviewed, only a handful reported that they considered their adviser a mentor. Faculty members do not receive any Brownie points for directing theses and dissertations. The tenure system is based largely on the prestige of research, publications, and faculty grants.

Department guidelines. Your first step is to get the department's handouts on selecting an adviser and committee. You want to know when to select an adviser, and how many faculty members will make up your committee. The guidelines may contain information you don't know, such as a requirement that one of your committee members come from outside your department or university. Get guidelines, too, on the format of the thesis/dissertation itself, including the procedures for submitting the finished product to the dean's office, for microfilming, or for library storage.

Faculty track record as an adviser. Once you have an idea for a topic and have a faculty member in mind, you need to know his or her success rate as an adviser. Find out from other student advisees what the faculty member is like. If you can contact former students, ask them as well. They may be more candid in their assessments of a professor's qualifications as an adviser. How often do these students meet with their advisers? Do they pass along chapters in progress or does the adviser want to see only the finished draft? How much responsibility does the adviser take in negotiating with other committee members? How involved is the adviser in working out conflicting suggestions or disagreements among committee members?

From the department you should also find out the average time to degree stats of advisees, the placement record of graduates under the adviser's supervision (how many students and where they got jobs), and the drop-out rate for advisees.

If at all possible, find an adviser who wants to see work in progress. It's better to get feedback on a chapter-by-chapter basis than on an entire manuscript. You want to deal with potential problems as they arise, rather than backtracking once you've completed and written your research.

Recommendations from the chair. You may also want to ask your department chair for input about potential advisers. It's never a bad idea to select a faculty adviser who gets along well with the chair. Such an adviser can facilitate progress on your degree and will work with the chair as necessary to resolve minor but time-consuming administrative obstacles. The department chair may be more motivated to help you solve larger problems if he or she has a good working and personal relationship with your adviser.

Faculty model. Who do you want to be when you "grow up"? A good rule of thumb is to select an adviser who closely matches your own ideal of an academic professional. Professors with whom you have a good personal rapport are obviously going to be attractive choices, but you want to balance a "warm and fuzzy" relationship with admiration and respect for their intellectual abilities. Your best choices would be seasoned professionals who are well-regarded in the field not only for their academic achievements but also for their positive interaction with colleagues. The best adviser will be a teacher as well as a friend.

Faculty plans and projects. With a few professors in mind, you now need to find out the nitty-gritty details about their schedules. It's a good idea to know their travel plans   will they be available during the summers? Do they have any long-term commitments to other projects off campus? In addition, get an idea of their current workload. You may want to work with the department chair, but keep in mind the heavy administrative responsibilities that go along with the job. I know one student whose adviser is her department chair, and they get together only once a year! In determining the faculty members' workload, also take into account such factors as the number of students they are currently advising and whether or not they are working on a large or time-consuming project, such as a book or grant project.

Selecting committee members. Once you've found an adviser who meets your criteria, your best bet in picking committee members is to get his or her suggestions. If you pick committee members without sounding out your choices with your adviser, you could end up with a

Be extremely careful about choosing an adviser. The type of adviser you select should match the type of person you are. If you decide you have the wrong type of adviser, attempting to change can put you in a very delicate situation. For one, grad students are an asset to faculty members. An offended past adviser can severely hamper your progress toward getting your degree. And finally, remember that you will eventually be that person's colleague. The world of researchers and academicians is still so small that your paths will inevitably cross. It is no good to have a feud started with others in your field before you even get your degree.

—Todd, Ph.D. student, Computer Engineering

If you use an outside reviewer as one of your committee members, make sure your adviser not only knows the outside faculty member but also respects (and, if possible, has a friendly relationship with) him or her.

contentious group. You want to ensure that there will be no hostility or political tensions among committee members. Your adviser will most often pick faculty members he or she can work with amicably. If your adviser's choices do not seem to cover the range of expertise you feel you need for your topic, politely ask, "What about so-and-so? I thought that he or she might have some good input to offer on methodology/theory/whatever." Pay close attention to the adviser's response, both verbal and nonverbal cues. If the professor hesitates, or offers lukewarm or clichéd praise of the faculty member you suggest, reconsider. You're getting a clue that the adviser does not feel he or she can work well with this professor.

THE PROPOSAL

With your adviser and committee members secured, you're ready to begin working on your proposal (also called a prospectus). You will be going to your adviser during the planning stages of the proposal to get advice on narrowing and focusing your topic. You should start by getting copies of recently accepted proposals. The graduate director, department AA's, or your adviser can provide you with good examples.

The structural arrangement of your proposal may vary. Offered below is a common format for students in the sciences or social sciences, but humanities students will also find it helpful. The design of this model is conveniently formulaic and broken down into manageable sections:

- Cover page
- Abstract
- Statement of the problem, including
    Introduction: nature of the problem, significance, what your results contribute
    Theoretical orientation
    Research question and subsidiary questions
    Limitations of study
- Summary

- Review of the literature
- Procedure (also called research methodology or design)
- Trial table of contents, if applicable
- Short bibliography

In the annotated bibliography at the back of this book you will find resources to help you put together each section of your thesis/dissertation proposal. Here are a few strategies for improving the proposal's overall quality.

Conduct a pilot study. One way to make your proposal stronger is to conduct a pilot or preliminary study, the results of which can be incorporated into your argument. Not only does a preliminary study add credibility to your proposal, but in working directly with the instruments, data, and techniques, you may be able to see potential problems and take steps to resolve them prior to starting the full project.

Take related classes. Another good piece of advice is to take as many statistics or programming courses as you need to gain a better grasp of data analysis and representation. Even though you may be employing a statistician or programmer, ultimately you are responsible for interpreting your data. And to communicate effectively, you need to have a working knowledge of the statistician's or programmer's duties, expertise, and lingo.

Include sample charts/tables. Even though you have not yet gathered the data for your study, your proposal will look more professional if you include samples of the kinds of diagrams you will be using to represent the data. This will demonstrate to the committee not only your long-range planning and organizational skills but also your familiarity with data collection, analysis, and representation.

Prepare a time line. It's very difficult to know exactly how long your thesis/dissertation will take. But your proposal should include a time line for the thesis/dissertation that is as realistic as possible. Find out first from your adviser, committee members, graduate director, and other students the average time it takes to complete a thesis/dissertation in the department. You can use these statistics as a general guide. Barbara

DO YOUR PROPOSAL IN STYLE

Find out from the department guidelines what style guide to use—MLA, Turabian, APA, etc.—and follow the same format in your proposal. Simple mechanical errors give faculty a negative impression, leading them to evaluate the substantive portions of your proposal more critically.

KEEP YOUR TIME LINE CURRENT

Once you begin working on the thesis/dissertation, update your personal time line based on the real time it takes to complete sections of your thesis/dissertation. Reevaluate your end date as necessary. The proposal time line should be integrated into your daily scheduling calendar throughout the thesis/dissertation process.

GIVE YOUR COMMITTEE ADVANCE COPIES OF YOUR PROPOSAL

Be sure to give your adviser and committee members plenty of time to review your proposal before the formal meeting. I would suggest giving them a couple of weeks. If you give them more time, your proposal may go into a "To-Do" pile and be forgotten until half an hour before the meeting is scheduled.

Cheshire's book, *The Best Dissertation . . . A Finished Dissertation (Or Thesis)*, offers a sample time line of about one to two years to complete a dissertation, including time spent researching and identifying your topic. When you begin planning your time line, be sure to consider (but not list) all of your responsibilities, not just work directly pertaining to your thesis or dissertation. If you have a full-time job or teaching load greater than that of other students, it's going to take longer.

REVIEW OF THE PROPOSAL

The proposal review will probably be the first formal meeting you have with your adviser and committee members. The meeting may be set by you, but more commonly your adviser will be responsible for the scheduling. From your adviser, find out how long the meeting is expected to last, and be sure to go over your finished proposal with your adviser beforehand to ask any questions. Your adviser should be able to give you an idea of what to expect in the meeting so you won't walk in unprepared. Get to the meeting room early to give yourself a chance to settle in and relax.

Also, make sure a memo is circulated, either by you or your adviser, to all involved regarding the time and place to meet of your proposal review meeting. Circulate the memo once just after the meeting has been scheduled, and again as a reminder a few days before the actual meeting.

The meeting itself is an excellent trial run for the oral defense. Although it will be less formal than the actual defense, it gives you a good idea of how everyone operates as a team. You will see how they work together (or don't) to solve problems, what aspects of your argument each tends to criticize the most, and how they respond when you defend your ideas. This is your first experience of group critique, and if you establish yourself as a colleague rather than a student, you can expect professional behavior from your committee that will continue throughout the thesis/dissertation process.

AFTER YOUR PROPOSAL IS ACCEPTED

You still have a few loose ends to tie up even after the committee has okayed your proposal. Many times a proposal is considered a contract between you, the committee, and/or the university. Find out to what extent the proposal is written in stone. You should be allowed flexibility to redraw conclusions based on unexpected data results, to modify your time line, and to add or change procedures as necessary. You may also want to ask your adviser, privately, what your responsibilities will be if any of the committee members resign or retire or if conflicts should arise that require you to replace any committee members. The department and university regulations may specify procedures on some of these points. It's important for you to have contingency plans if anything comes up that forces you to make changes either in your proposal or your committee.

WRITING: ORGANIZATIONAL STRATEGIES

Begin a thesis/dissertation notebook. In essence, you are writing a book about your topic. It may be a short book if you're writing a thesis, or it may be a full-length book if you're writing a dissertation. Regardless, it's important to think of your thesis or dissertation as a bona fide manuscript. I recommend using a three-ring notebook with tabs to divide your chapters. You may also want to include a section for memos or notes on meetings.

Outline each chapter. The usual procedure for drafting a chapter outline is to do a lot of research, type notes into the computer, and then organize them into an outline form. I recommend a different strategy. After

Don't rush to select an adviser. TA for faculty you're considering as committee members. Choosing big names is tempting, but they'll have the least time to evaluate your work as you go along. I think it's better to choose people who are enthusiastic about your work and you, who can make sure you are getting your work done on schedule without intimidating you. I went for a balance of junior faculty members who have loads of energy, enthusiasm, and new ideas, and senior faculty who have a reputation in the field.

—Karen, Ph.D. student, Modern Thought and Literature

DRAFT DODGING

Keep only your latest draft of a chapter in the notebook. Unless you want reams of paper cluttering up your office, I would suggest filing away earlier drafts—you'll probably never look at them again once you've done the next rewrite. You may refer to these earlier drafts when you're preparing chapters for publication. Chances are, however, you'll end up throwing them out.

you've done considerable reading or data gathering, write an outline off the top of your head, without first referring to your notes. During phases of intense concentration on your research, a chapter outline seems to gel more or less subconsciously. You can use notes afterward to fill in any gaps. Usually, however, you will have taken more notes than you need and will end up cutting excessive references and irrelevant data.

While researching one chapter, you'll often run across references that you can use in writing later chapters. Store such information in your manuscript notebook as soon as you find it. When you are ready to write up that next chapter, you've already started compiling information for an outline. It's much less intimidating to write the next chapter when you already have a stack of information to get you started.

Know your audience. Any writer knows the importance of his or her audience. Remember: Even though you may intend to publish parts or all of your thesis/dissertation, right now you're writing just for your committee. You want to modify your organization and writing style to meet their expectations as much as possible without compromising elements of your argument. If committee members tend to use short, concise sentences, do the same. If they emphasize detail in their own work, provide plenty of support for your points. If they focus heavily on theoretical implications of certain procedures and methods, be sure to address them in your own work. Principally you're writing for your adviser, so matching your thesis/dissertation to his or her methodology and presentation style should take precedence over the personal styles of other committee members.

Cite counterarguments. What's the best way to respond to criticism? Anticipate it. Your committee's job is to find holes in your argument. Your job is to support and defend your position, and one way to do this is to include opposing views and defeat them. You will almost certainly be doing this verbally in the oral defense. If you've prepared for it in the writing of your thesis/dissertation, you will be able to defend your position by referring back to your written text.

Give your committee polished drafts. Presentation is everything. You never want to give your committee anything that doesn't look like a finished product. Each draft should have a cover page with the thesis/dissertation and chapter title, your name, date submitted, and any other information that would usually go on the cover page of the final thesis/dissertation. Students submitting a full draft of the entire thesis/dissertation will usually bind the draft together like a book. You may not be the most able typist on the word processor, but you should use features like the spell checker and grammar checker to make your draft as neat as possible. If you need additional help, English tutors or the campus Writing Center can review your drafts before you submit them. If the appearance of your draft looks neat and professional, the committee will take your argument—and you—more seriously.

WRITING: PSYCHOLOGICAL STRATEGIES

The Doubting Thomas/Thomasina Syndrome. Getting down in the dumps about a thesis/dissertation is universal. When it happens, remember that it happens to everybody—getting the blues about your project is an intrinsic feature of the project itself. You may worry that you won't ever finish the writing or that your topic is boring or insignificant. Sometimes in reviewing the literature you will find a dissertation or article you think already proves or disproves your argument. You'll have periods where you get writer's block or you may become demoralized when your data doesn't match your hypothesis or conclusions.

Some students will speculate morbidly about their chances on the job market (see Chapter 10 for more on this). Others will look around at their fellow students and compare their own progress unfavorably, or look at their fellow students and feel isolated and lonely by comparison. Doubts about the home front may surface

I picked my dissertation committee and chair because they knew how to deliver critical feedback positively and constructively. My friends, by contrast, selected advisers and committee members based on the content area and expertise of these individuals, paying little or no regard to their social skills (or lack thereof) and scientific orientations. While my oral exams and dissertation writing process have been intellectually stimulating and rewarding, their experiences have been frustrating in the extreme. One friend had a committee member openly shout at and berate him during an oral defense session.

—Daniel, Ph.D. student, Social Psychology

DOUBTS ABOUT YOUR COMMITTEE, TOO

It's not uncommon for students to have periods of resentment toward their committees. Students may feel like slaves—or overly obedient children—for conceding to every demand of a faculty member.

when students think they're getting too old to continue or fear they're losing touch with their families and communities.

All of these doubts are normal. At least, normal within the context of writing a thesis or dissertation. (Psychologists could argue that the demands of a thesis or dissertation are unhealthy for just these reasons!) Here are a couple of tips for managing this kind of stress so you can get back to the project at hand.

Recognize when you're escaping. Many, many of these doubts are the products of avoidance. If you're stuck at a point in your dissertation research, you will be tempted to step back from the whole process rather than digging in to deal with a specific obstacle. Waxing philosophical (and bitter) about the thesis/dissertation process justifies procrastination. You may have a legitimate concern that a committee member is being overly critical of your writing. Or you may be using that excuse to keep from having to think through his or her suggestions for significant changes.

Then tackle the problem. If you see that you're avoiding work by pondering negative fears, you're more than half way to solving the real problem. If your obstacle happens to be data results that don't support your hypothesis, be flexible. Let the data itself speak to you and see what new conclusions you find, or what incorrect assumptions you may have made in your original hypothesis. Remember how many inventors have contributed major scientific achievements while working on an unrelated project! Let your adviser know of the problems you're having with the data, and he or she can help you modify your argument from the original proposal. In her book, *The Best Dissertation . . . A Finished Dissertation (Or Thesis)*, Barbara Cheshire tells her own story of not finding the statistical significance in her study that she predicted in her hypothesis. Since then, she has written articles and given talks on her erroneous assumptions about the data and contributed new knowledge to her field.

Break down your work. If the problem is something less specific, such as a mental or writing block, you may be thinking of (and fearing) the project as a whole rather than breaking it down into manageable components.

Think of the thesis/dissertation as a series of papers. You've probably written a 20-page paper for class in a month's time with no problem. When you're writing chapters, write them as self-contained papers. You can go back and edit to add transitions that link one chapter to another. And, no matter what kind of perfectionist you are, it's perfectly okay for you to write garbage, so long as you're writing something. When I feel less than creative, I'll often write in a conversational tone what I'm trying to say, even if it's not very clear to me. Usually after a page or two the real ideas start kicking in and the writing begins to flow. Afterward, it's easy to edit out the rambling material.

Stop reading. Most students don't know when to quit with a literature review. They're always worried that the next journal article or book may contain the key piece of information. Or they may keep checking references to make sure no one has published their arguments. You may think you're being a thorough and diligent researcher. In reality, you're trying to put off doing your own thinking and writing. At some point, you've got to stop and get on with your own work. Even when another dissertation or article discusses the same topic, the writer won't have your same approach or analytical take on the material. You know from having the proposal accepted that your work is valuable, interesting, and relevant. Once you've finished writing your thesis/ dissertation, you can always go back to the library and update your research. If you find anything relevant, in most cases all you need to do is include a footnote.

Get counseling. Many students say they could not have made it through their dissertations without a therapist. When psychological doubts arise, a therapist is invaluable for providing you with coping skills. Many times the students who are the most driven and outwardly successful need therapy the most. If you're a perfectionist (and most of us are or we wouldn't be here) you'll be overjoyed to learn that it's okay if you can't give 100 percent to everything at all times.

A therapist can also help separate your personal needs from your professional ambitions. Sometimes the overly diligent student neglects his or her own well-being—many can't say "no" to another project for fear of losing their status as a top student in a program. You

I finally finished my dissertation on topic #3—I wasted about three years on topics #1 and #2. It's critical that you identify your strengths and weaknesses early on and drop a topic quickly if it isn't working out. When you begin thinking about a topic, your first priority should be what my adviser calls "proof of concept," a demonstration that this idea will work for you. Only after you have established this first consideration can you focus on the second-order problems.

—John, Ph.D. graduate, Zoology

You will usually know the difference intuitively between a concern that needs to be addressed and needless worries that surface when you are avoiding the work. Ask yourself honestly why you're worried about this particular issue right now. Chances are you'll see that the real fear is a specific dissertation problem and that getting to work will ameliorate your anxiety.

may be able to find balance (and peace of mind) in your day-to-day living with the help of therapeutic techniques.

Join a support group. Your department may already have some kind of doctoral seminar or thesis/dissertation colloquium in place. If not, you may want to form your own. Getting together with four or five students on a regular basis not only stimulates you intellectually but also contributes to your emotional health. You can offer, and will no doubt receive, emotional encouragement along with valuable suggestions on your research. If you join a group, the other members should be in your same general field. You may not want to be in a group where one member is working on a very similar project. Sometimes the competitive instinct can overrule the desire for a free association of ideas. You or the other student may be less inclined to admit weaknesses or ask for needed help. And make sure that all members of the group distribute a handout or present an outline of their project.

Take a break? Would you rather spend two weeks in Key West or finish your chapter? This is a rhetorical question, of course. We all know we'd be on the plane tomorrow! You need periodic breaks in your work to see friends, be with your family, and relax. But the key to relaxing for a longer break is proper timing. Make sure you take a break only if you've reached a stopping point in your work. If you drop your work in the middle of analyzing a chunk of data, revising a chapter, or preparing a survey, it will plague you the whole time you're on your break. This is the voice of experience talking! You need the vacations—not enough students take them—but they need to be planned between stages in your work. Finish the chapter, compile your notes on the data, have that last meeting with your adviser. Then take off.

WRITING: COMMITTEE STRATEGIES

You'll graduate a lot sooner if relations with your adviser and committee run smoothly and professionally.

The relationship you form with them should not be that of student to teacher, or child to parent, but colleague to colleague. Begin your relationship with the adviser and committee as an academic professional right from the start.

Schedule regular meetings. Your adviser's responsibilities do not include scheduling regular meetings—that's your job. Try to schedule meetings, if possible, every four to six weeks with your adviser. You will probably meet less frequently with other committee members. Arrange meetings with all parties together as necessary. Schedule meetings for at least half an hour, and don't plan anything afterward in case the discussion goes on longer. Before you go into a meeting, have a plan for it. Submit a chapter or request a draft back from the faculty member, ask questions, write down answers. If you have a poor memory or don't take comprehensive notes, tape meetings with permission from the faculty members. Try to keep meeting times and places consistent.

Avoid meetings over the phone, if possible. You need to be physically present in the department on a regular basis to forestall that "lost sheep" feeling common to students working in isolation.

Document everything (or "CYA"). Your working relationship with the committee should be as formal as that in any other office environment. This means that you need to keep track, in writing, of everything that goes on to protect yourself from verbal misunderstandings. Draft regular progress reports of your meetings, including date, time, topics discussed, decisions reached, draft submitted or returned, plans for incorporating (or reasons for not incorporating) revisions, and the date and time of a subsequent meeting. If committee members agree to it, distribute memos of meetings with individual members to the entire committee. You may want to ask that the committee member sign off on the memo once it's received. If a committee member verbally disagrees or wants to modify the content of your memo, make sure you document and circulate his or her request for changes.

Defend your ideas. There's a fine line between defense and defensiveness. The fact that the committee

SOME PRACTICAL ADVICE

The more you fight suggestions from your committee, the longer you'll stay in school and the more money you'll spend. It doesn't affect your committee or adviser one way or another how much pondering and soul-searching you do. Remember that your goal is to finish school and get your degree.

accepted your proposal means you're on firm ground to defend your procedures, hypothesis, and literature review. It's a good idea to rehearse a few neutral comments if you anticipate criticism of any of these items: "I chose this procedure because . . ." or "I believe these instruments will yield the most comprehensive data on X" or "I'm not sure that the literature review on this issue would support my topic as strongly as the research I've already done on Y." Having a few canned statements will keep you from getting emotionally heated over their criticisms. If objections are minor, don't fight them. But if a criticism is major, think about it for awhile before you agree or disagree. If you have a week's time to ponder the problem—and distance yourself from the sting of criticism—you may see that taking the suggestions will make your thesis/dissertation even stronger.

Separate yourself from your work. Many students doing major writing projects for the first time tend to treat them as their children. They may get too emotionally involved with their topics and become irrational when changes are suggested. In truth, your thesis/dissertation is not yours alone—it is a collaborative project. If you can treat your project as a combined effort, even when the committee suggests major revisions to your argument, you'll save yourself from countless headaches and pent-up hostility. You're not giving in, but working within the system to reach your goal—getting that degree.

Responding to conflicting suggestions. It's very common for committee members to offer radically opposing suggestions for revision. Many times your adviser will help you resolve conflicting suggestions among committee members. One strategy you can use is to respond to minor suggestions without really dealing with the major ones. Often, if faculty members see that some of their ideas have been incorporated, they'll literally forget about the rest of their objections. Your committee members want to feel that they are being heard—you can give them something, but not everything, and still make them happy.

Also, you may find a series of "What about X?" or "Have you considered the implications of Y?" written on your draft. Committee members often suggest changes off the top of their heads without really thinking through them. They expect you to consider the question and evaluate its suitability to your argument. Remember that the committee members are probably not wedded to their suggestions—don't treat them like commandments.

COMMON COMMITTEE PROBLEMS (AND SOLUTIONS)

Here are a few suggestions for handling some of the sticky situations that may arise.

Personality conflicts. If you did the background research on prospective advisers and committee members, you shouldn't have this problem. Occasionally, however, a faculty member will be very nice and supportive of you in the beginning, but will become your nemesis as the project gets underway. Common personality problems include sexism, jealousy, and criticism of your work without offering a justifiable rationale or possible solutions.

Taping your meetings is an effective way to handle these problems. You can argue that you want to tape meetings to write up more accurate progress reports and memos. If they resist, ask why, or ask for alternate suggestions. And deal with any personal problems as soon as they arise; you've got to maintain your relationship on a professional footing.

You may have to go to your adviser with the problem, but if at all possible, don't go over a committee member's head to the administration. Try to resolve any personal problems on your own through professional channels—by taping meetings, writing up meetings, distributing notes to the whole committee, and by limiting opportunities for argumentative committee members to harass you in private.

Intellectual game-players. The university is full of professors who like to chew over an idea or play devil's advocate just for fun. These folks undoubtedly have too

HANDLING PROBLEM PROFESSORS

Keep thesis/dissertation meetings limited to prescheduled times with all of your committee members. Don't drop in on troublesome committee members or allow them to chat informally with you inside or outside the office—that's inviting conflict.

A CAVEAT ABOUT RELATIONSHIPS

Getting romantically involved with your adviser is a great way to sabotage your career. Everyone finds out, sooner or later, and nasty comments from students and faculty will be directed at you, not your adviser. This negative perception of your relationship will also effectively cut off any networking channels in the department. Suddenly you're out of the loop.

much time on their hands! If you end up with one of these, you don't have to throw up your hands in despair. You can usually steer professors away from idle speculation by getting them to answer their own questions. To get back to the main point you may ask them how exploring this topic contributes to the overall project.

Perhaps the best advice for these game-players is to bore them to death with details. Usually these professors just like toying with an idea in its abstract form and resist dealing with specific details. You can behave as if you're seriously trying to address their questions, and start speculating out loud about how many extra pages their ideas will add to the dissertation and other specifics of investigating this issue—what instruments would be needed, what time would need to be scheduled in the lab, what literature sources would be a good place to start, what issues you might also want to address that tangentially relate to their ideas, and so on. Whenever applicable, bring up the specter of additional costs. If you bombard the game-player with planning details and nit-picky scheduling issues, you take the fun out of the game, and, hopefully, he or she will let it go.

"Personal" relationships. The goal of your relationship with your committee is not to be liked but respected. This is an important distinction. Sometimes, because a student will be working so closely with an adviser, a relationship will form that goes beyond professional boundaries. Most times these relationships end in disaster for the student involved. Four years or more is a long time to maintain an intimate relationship (just check out divorce statistics), and the student is always the losing party if the relationship breaks up.

Breaking up is hard to do. Despite all of your best efforts, you may realize that you have to replace your adviser or one of your committee members. You should know the department or university policy on replacing committee members, but you should try to make your change as informally and discreetly as possible. Find a good, nonpersonal reason for replacing a faculty member and discuss it with him or her privately. The "irreconcilable difference" should always be research-oriented rather than personal or political. If the faculty member already recognizes there's a problem between you, he or she will probably be grateful for the change. The professor may not want to work with you any more than you want to work with him or her. If your relationship is more amicable, you and the faculty member can work together to find a replacement.

Even though the department chair is usually required to be involved in any change of committee members, don't rush to your chair before you've tried to resolve the problem on your own or with your adviser. Go to your chair with the solution, not the problem. Alternately, let your adviser work with the chair. Department chairs are overworked as it is, and despite their obligation to oversee the situation, they honestly would prefer not to get entangled in disputes of this kind.

TEN THINGS NOT TO DO OR SAY AT YOUR THESIS DEFENSE

1. Describe parts of your thesis using interpretive dance.
2. "And it would have worked if it weren't for those meddling kids. . . ."
3. Use a Greek chorus to highlight important points.
4. "You call THAT a question? How the **** did they make you a professor?"
5. Lead the spectators in the Wave.
6. "I don't know—I didn't write this."
7. The Emperor's New Slides ("Only fools can't see the writing. . . .")
8. "I could answer that, but then I'd have to kill you."
9. Challenge a professor to a duel. Slapping him with a glove is optional.
10. "Anybody else as drunk as I am?"

—From "150 Things Not to Do or Say at Your Thesis Defense," by Peter Dutton, Jim Lalopoulos, and Alison Berube (http://www.naples.net/~nfn02644)

THE ORAL DEFENSE

Once you've incorporated the suggestions for the final chapters from your committee, you're ready to

Early in my studies I began to work with a man who did research in an area that interested me greatly. Over the years my personal life got more intertwined with his—I worked as a reader for his classes, did research assignments for him, used his homes when he was away, took care of his pets. I knew that I was useful to him outside our purely professional relationship, but figured I could use the relationship to benefit myself as well. After several years I realized I was terribly wrong about this relationship, that instead it was damaging to me both personally and professionally.

—Dee, Ph.D. student, Sociology

REPLACING A COMMITTEE MEMBER

If you want to replace a committee member rather than your adviser, you can go to your adviser with the problem and see if he or she can recommend a diplomatic solution. As with your discussions with the faculty member involved, don't give personal reasons for making a change, even if the problem is personal. Many times your adviser will be aware of the real reason without you having to spell it out.

submit the completed dissertation for oral defense. An oral defense will probably not be required of master's students for their theses. If it is, the defense will almost always be a formality rather than a substantive review.

For most programs, the adviser will schedule the oral defense in a seminar room. Your committee will be there, and a couple of faculty members will usually be asked to participate as outside readers and evaluators of your dissertation and defense. Frequently, an oral defense is open to anyone who wishes to attend.

You will generally begin the defense by giving a short presentation that summarizes your dissertation. Then your committee and outside readers will begin asking you specific questions. The oral defense only lasts about 2 hours, and at the end you will be asked to wait outside while the committee votes on whether to pass your dissertation and defense.

Most schools treat an oral defense as a rubber stamp of your dissertation, making you go through the tension and doubt of one last hurdle, even though they fully intend to pass you. Still, you shouldn't walk in expecting an unconditional pass. A committee that goes to the trouble of looking over your work one last time and meeting in a formal setting will generally want to have something to show for the time it has expended. Thus, it's very common for the committee to pass you with minor changes. Not all programs, however, treat the oral defense so lightly; and the Fail option is a possibility at any school. Find out from other students how the defense is most often handled by your department.

Having to defend your work out loud after spending years reading and writing about it may cause you some anxiety. Here are a few tips to keep your stress level to a minimum.

Know the procedures. Who is invited to attend your oral defense? You should know whether or not it is open to anyone so you can be prepared to address a larger audience. Also, find out from your adviser who the outside faculty readers will be. Do a little research on these professors before you go into the defense. Ask their students about their personalities and read a few of their publications if you have time. This will give you a feel for their research concentration and methodology, political slants, and writing style. With a little background on them, you may be able to anticipate the kinds of questions they will ask.

Prepare a good abstract. In his book, *How to Complete and Survive a Doctoral Dissertation*, David Sternberg claims that it is not uncommon for outside readers, and even your committee members, to read only parts of your dissertation prior to the defense. The outside faculty members may have been requested to serve on the defense committee at the last minute. For this reason, the abstract should contain a clear presentation of your whole argument—thesis statement, procedures, conclusions, and, most importantly, how your work contributes to the profession. It's possible that faculty questions may come mainly from your abstract if readers haven't had time to give your dissertation a full review. The abstract should attempt to answer their questions before they ask them.

Use visual aids. Because you will probably be required to get the ball rolling by doing a short presentation of your work, it's a good idea to include visual aids. Not only will aids draw attention away from your anxiety-ridden face, but they also make you look more professional to the committee, as if you're preparing a talk for a conference or a class. Many students simply use the blackboard, but if you have more time, you may want to prepare handouts, slides, or materials for an overhead. If you use visual aids, practice incorporating them into the presentation. If possible, practice in the room where the defense will be held. And make sure in advance that the projector, screen, or blackboard has been placed in the meeting room.

Prepare answers to commonly asked questions. You can't know in advance exactly what a committee will ask, but there are a few standard questions that usually come up. You can think about and practice responding to them. Common questions include the following.

- Why did you choose X procedure(s)?
- If you could do your study again, what would you do differently?
- Were there any weaknesses in using X approach?
- Discuss your major findings.

VOTING OPTIONS FOR THE ORAL DEFENSE

- Unconditional pass
- Pass with minor revisions
- Pass with major revisions
- Fail (either defense, dissertation, or both)

- How would your study make a contribution to classroom teaching?
- What are your plans for future research on this topic (where would you go from here)?

Your adviser may be able to suggest other questions that frequently come up. It's a good idea, if you can, to locate former students of any of the faculty members on the defense committee to get an indication of the kinds of questions they've asked during defenses of other dissertations.

Fielding a tough question. Despite your preparation, you will always get one or two questions that seem to come out of left field. They may be unclearly stated, irrelevant, or so expansive that a thorough answer would take half an hour. I recommend a little subterfuge here. Remember in college when a kid asked a question and the professor seemed to answer a totally different question? A simple misunderstanding? Maybe, but more likely the professor didn't know the answer and chose to answer a question of his or her own construction.

You can do this, too, although it has to be more subtle. Try to bring the question back to the firm ground of your research. You may respond with, "Ah, I see what you're asking, and I considered this question when I was analyzing my data on X. My results suggested. . . ." There's a good chance that you can field the question this way. The faculty member, while probably frustrated, will realize that the only way to get a straight answer is to redirect the question to an issue specifically related to the dissertation. Hopefully, rather than having to rethink the question, the professor will just nod and you can move on.

CAN YOU FAIL?

It's extremely rare for a student to fail the oral defense. Because the adviser and committee members have directed your dissertation throughout the research and writing, they should not want you to fail. After all, it's a poor reflection on them to have one of their students fail an oral defense. Sternberg states that some students may occasionally fail their oral defense but pass their dissertations. In such a case you can retake the oral portion if necessary. For those two or three students I interviewed who failed the defense and theses/dissertation, the failure was always the result of a falling out with their advisers. If you've selected your adviser and committee members carefully, you won't fail.

WHEN YOU PASS

Although some students rush out immediately to a bar and pound shots of Cuervo, other students face a kind of postpartum depression when it's all over. If you're one of the latter, give yourself a few days to let the news settle in and the trauma subside. Then celebrate! Have a party or take a trip with your family. Your department will probably offer a reception for its new graduates, a time when you will be celebrated as an equal by your fellow faculty members. This can be especially rewarding after years of toil on your dissertation. Don't miss the chance to be patted on the back.

I want to offer an additional suggestion to "spread the wealth" of your new status. Ask the department or the grad student organization to host a party just for supportive "others"—friends, parents, partners, and children who have helped students make it through the degree process. While you deserve to be in the spotlight after years of hard work, it can be additionally gratifying to recognize as real contributors to your degree those patient folks who have supported you. And they will adore being recognized, not just by you but by the whole department! This is a great way to feel a sense of contentment and closure about the entire grad school process.

CHAPTER 9
CONFERENCES AND PUBLISHING

How to Write Good

1. *Avoid alliteration. Always.*
2. *Prepositions are not words to end sentences with.*
3. *Avoid clichés like the plague. (They're old hat.)*
4. *Eschew ampersands & abbreviations, etc.*
5. *Parenthetical remarks (however relevant) are unnecessary.*
6. *Foreign words and phrases are not apropos.*
7. *Eliminate quotations. As Ralph Waldo Emerson said, "I hate quotations. Tell me what you know."*
8. *Comparisons are as bad as clichés.*
9. *Be more or less specific.*
10. *Analogies in writing are like feathers on a snake.*
11. *The passive voice is to be avoided.*
12. *Go around the barn at high noon to avoid colloquialisms.*
13. *Even if a mixed metaphor sings, it should be derailed.*
14. *Who needs rhetorical questions?*
15. *Exaggeration is a billion times worse than understatement.*

—Sally Bulford, from Laughweb (http://www.misty.com/laughweb/education)

Presenting at conferences and publishing research are often referred to as "CV fodder." You're racking up credentials for the job search. As you begin to present and publish your research, you gradually move out of the nurturing confines of your department and into the larger academic arena.

Being successful in this extended community requires you to demonstrate a variety of talents beyond good research skills. You have to know which topics are marketable for conferences and publication, how to mold your writing to particular audiences, how to speak well in public, even how to schmooze over cocktails with folks you've never met. In essence, you're learning to make an impression that goes beyond raw intellectual ability. You're marketing your scholarship and yourself.

CONFERENCES

The purpose of conferences is to promote research that has yet to be published. Students and faculty write up or post their current research and bounce ideas off other respected researchers in the same field. Many students and faculty present their research as a prelude to publishing it. They incorporate comments and suggestions from the conference audience and submit the finished product to academic journals. In some cases they run into editors in the audience who want to publish their papers right away. Conferencing is also a form of personal networking. You may find that your intellectual hero will be attending a particular conference, and you want to present a paper in hopes of meeting him or her.

WHEN SHOULD YOU START?

Yesterday! It's never too early to begin attending conferences. I once presented a paper from a class that I took in my second quarter of grad school. This was very early compared to my peers, but it got me into the academic stream that much sooner and gave me

I have electronically published my dissertation and one other manuscript on-line via the World Wide Web. I am convinced more individuals will actually read the work there than if I published it in some erudite but obscure peer-reviewed psychology journal. WWW statistics show that others are reading my work every month.

—Neil, Ph.D. graduate, Psychology

JOB NETWORKING

It's very common for students who are preparing for a job search to target conferences where they might make good job contacts. They may attend a large, prestigious conference or one attended by faculty from schools in which they're interested.

professional experience that has contributed to my grad school success. I made contacts in my first year of grad school that I couldn't have made any other way. And I got a chance to see, before I had decided on my research area, what kinds of topics were getting the most attention from scholars.

FINDING CONFERENCES

This is the easiest part of the conference process. You'll find CFPs (Calls for Papers) everywhere—they are ubiquitous in academe. Joining a professional organization is a good way to find out about conferences in specialized areas. Associations usually publish a newsletter listing CFPs for both large national and smaller regional conferences. Your department will receive CFPs and post them on the department's bulletin board. You can also find out about conferences very quickly on the Internet. There's a gopher site exclusively dedicated for CFPs in literature. It's updated regularly and comprehensive in scope. Most fields have a similar site or Web page listing of CFPs. If you've subscribed to an Internet discussion group in your field, you'll see CFPs regularly posted on-line. Usually the CFP will include the date and location of an upcoming conference as well as the details and guidelines for submitting, for example, providing just the abstract or the completed paper.

START WITH A SMALL OR LARGE CONFERENCE?

You may want to select a local or smaller conference for your first presentation. A local conference means you'll spend a lot less money on travel expenses. My first conference was a long way from home, but it was a smaller, specialized conference. And it was the best conference I've ever attended. Because it was smaller, I met just about everyone there. We all ate lunch together, took walks around the grounds and enjoyed dinner and cocktails together. The conference committee was able to provide excellent entertainment for us because we were a small group. It was cozy, intimate, collegial rather than competitive, a real treat for my first time out.

A smaller conference also helps build confidence for a larger audience. If you make mistakes, a smaller audience may be more forgiving just because of its intimacy. You can go to cocktails with the rest of the panel members after a presentation, and invite the audience along. It may not be as intimidating because most of the well-known scholars tend to go to the larger gatherings.

On the other hand, if you've got an incredible topic and want to go for gold, you can submit it to the larger, national conferences. The exposure to a large conference environment is good practice, though nerve-racking. It may also be more difficult to meet people and network at a larger conference. It's up to you to seek out and hobnob with the big guns who are attending.

CHICKEN OR THE EGG?

There are two ways to submit your work to a conference. You can either send in an abstract of a paper you would like to write, or you can send in a finished paper (or abstract of a finished paper). Though established faculty members may get away with doing only an abstract, for beginners I suggest writing the paper first and then shopping around for a conference.

PREPARING AN ABSTRACT

Many conference panels require only an abstract of your presentation to make a decision. Abstract writing is very different from writing the formal paper. It's basically a sales pitch to the panel chairperson, tailored to the panel's specific topic. Use department letterhead

I was giving my first conference paper and, understandably, was a bit nervous. The world authority on my subject, a friend of my adviser's, was attending the panel. My adviser asked this man to give me an easy ride and not to ask any awkward questions. While giving my talk I tried to look as nonchalant as possible. I was later described as being "so laid back I was nearly horizontal." The world expert came up to me afterward and said that having such an off-hand attitude, while not looking arrogant, was a trait that many people spend years cultivating.

—Connor, Ph.D. student, Computer Science

for your cover letter, and don't make your "pitch" any longer than a few paragraphs unless otherwise specified. I think shorter is better, and I always fit my abstract onto a single page of letterhead. The conference panel chairperson will usually want to know a little bit about you, too, so you can open with a paragraph stating your degree status and listing any publications or special projects that relate to the panel topic.

For my abstracts I use a standard three-paragraph format. If you use this approach, the first paragraph should read like the intro to your paper, usually discussing the background of the topic and its significance. The second paragraph deals specifically with the issues your paper addresses and the third states what kinds of conclusions the paper draws. In essence, you're giving the reader a short but engaging synopsis of your entire paper.

The abstract, needless to say, should contain your best writing, better even than your actual paper. I've spent an entire evening preparing a 250-word abstract for a conference, editing, rewriting, reading out loud, referring to my paper for word choices, and so on. Don't crank out your abstract at the last minute before the submission deadline. And remember that your purpose is to persuade the panel chairperson that your idea is current, interesting, and significant. If necessary, write in your draft, "This presentation is significant because . . ." and then rewrite the sentence later with more sophistication.

FROM CLASS PAPER TO CONFERENCE PRESENTATION

Students in the sciences will usually start by posting or presenting results from their accumulated lab research. For other students, however, class papers can provide the foundation of a good conference presentation. For classes most students will prepare final papers anywhere from 15 to 25 pages in length. No doubt your professors are encouraging you to dig into lesser-studied topics and come up with original research ideas. If your professors are training you well, they will say that you should treat any class paper as a potential article and use the same rigorous standards in selecting and writing about your topic. If you're not getting this advice, take it from me. I submitted four class papers to conferences or for publication while still a master's student. One was the very first paper I wrote in grad school. But these papers had to be modified substantially before they were ready for a conference or for publication. Here are a few suggestions for adapting a paper to a conference presentation.

Shorten the length. Most conferences will specify a time limit on your presentation, usually no longer than 20-25 minutes. I would recommend an even stricter time limit, no matter how fascinating the topic. Like most people, scholars' attention spans expire after about 15 minutes of continuous reading, no matter what kind of groundbreaking research is being offered. I've noticed that shorter papers, for whatever reason, seem to get more positive feedback. If scholars have questions or want more information, they can always address them in the Q&A session after the presentation.

Some students think that one page of double-spaced type equals one minute of talking. It doesn't. If you're talking a page per minute, you're going way too fast. Your paper needs to be cut down to 10 pages excluding notes and bibliography. This is especially tough to do, both for students and faculty. They seem convinced that their argument cannot be presented in 10 pages without having gaps in logic. All you need to do is let your audience know that your presentation highlights points of a longer paper on the subject. Offer copies of the completed paper to anyone who's interested in hearing more. Ten extra copies should be enough to provide for audience requests.

Cut out quotations/citations. Students writing class papers are taught, wisely, to include plenty of support for their arguments in the form of quotations and references to other sources. In a conference paper, this additional padding is not really necessary to your argument. You may want to include one or two citations from very prestigious scholars, to let people know that you've done your homework. But beyond that you're

DON'T OVERQUOTE

Quotes never get much attention from the audience. Many times they distract from the flow of the argument, like a digression or an aside. Remember that your audience will be specialized rather than general—they'll know the research territory without your having to describe it in detail.

LEAD CREED

A good presentation has a killer lead-in. Good conference papers do not begin, "The issue of X remains a controversial subject in contemporary scholarship . . ." This is how you begin a class paper, and such a formulaic approach is perfectly acceptable in a class context. However, to a conference audience, this is stating the obvious. Try to make your introductory paragraph an attention-getter and assume an authoritative tone throughout your paper.

wasting time. If the backup of having citations makes you feel more comfortable, include a separate list of quotations and sources to refer to during the Q&A session.

Add your own "voice." The biggest difference between the class paper and the conference paper or publication is tone. Most students are timid in asserting their individuality in a class paper and stick to a prescribed (read "dry") academic writing style. You can be a little more personal—and assertive about your points—in a conference paper. I know these are difficult qualities to define. All I can say is that the best conference papers I've seen include a little bit of humor or a relevant personal anecdote to warm up an audience. Play around with humor in your paper. Experiment with putting a little bit of yourself into your writing and see what you get. Chances are you'll end up with a paper that informs and engages your audience.

Shorten your sentences. Long, convoluted sentences seem to be the tacit norm of conference papers. But turgid prose is the death knell of a good idea, torture for the presenter and the audience. Grad students tend to use a lot of jargon in class papers to impress their professors. But there's an important distinction between technically sophisticated writing and obscure jargon.

The best way to clean up your convoluted prose is to shorten it. If you abbreviate a four line sentence to two lines, you'll clarify your argument. Read one of your longer sentences out loud and see how much breath it takes out of you. (This may be one of the reasons that quotes from other scholars don't go over well out loud; this kind of academic prose is intended to be read.)

FINANCIAL AID FOR CONFERENCE PARTICIPATION

Even my publicly funded state school, impoverished as it is, offers financial aid to students who attend conferences. It's not much, but I applied for every penny! Find out if your department offers financial aid and if other university sources of aid are available as well. I received money both from my department and from the student government association. The university may have some kind of program set up to help grad students defray travel expenses.

TRAVELING ON THE CHEAP

Because the departmental aid may not be substantial, you can use the following tips to save a few dollars on your travel expenses:

- Stay with family or friends in town instead of the hotel. You can also contact grad students at the local university to see if any students will let you stay with them. I prefer to stay in the hotel if I can afford it, just to be available to attend panels at will or meet people in the hotel lounge for cocktails or dinner. It's better to be in the thick of the action, but not always a possibility on a limited student budget.
- Advertise that you're seeking a roommate to split the costs of a hotel room. When you make your reservations, you'll notice that most hotels charge the same price for a room with one bed or two. Obviously it makes sense to find someone else to stay with you.
- Make your plane reservations early and find out about possible student travel discounts from your local travel agency.
- Don't fly. If practical, consider driving to the conference and sharing the drive with other conference participants.
- Don't attend the entire conference. Fly in the day you're presenting and fly back out the same day. This will save you money on hotel accommodations, but it may add to the stress factor (and the airfare cost). Also, you'll miss the opportunity to meet others outside your panel or participate in scheduled activities and entertainment. Weigh

My adviser called me into her office one term and said, "It is time for you to think about presenting and getting published." I was startled—it felt early to me. But she was right. The first time around my conference proposal was denied, but the next year it went through, and my adviser and I turned it into a publishable article. I was glad she pushed me, and I took her advice on publishing very seriously.

—Amanda, Ph.D. student, Education

SLIDES

If you use slides, it's a good idea to bring your own projector. Some conferences will provide it for you, but it's better if you have your own equipment. You don't want to have to learn how to operate it during the presentation!

this option carefully, especially if it's your first conference. I think it's better for a first conference to get a feel for the whole thing.

- Turn the conference into a vacation. Extending your trip for a few days or a week may cut down on airfare costs. Airlines make their money on business travelers who fly in and out of cities the same day. If you're already getting some conference funding from the university, the extra money may offset the cost of a longer hotel stay. And don't you deserve a vacation?

BUTTERFLIES BE GONE!

The first conference presentation is the hardest. After that, it gets much easier to stand up in front of strangers and read your paper. Here are a few ideas for preparing for the actual presentation and conquering the fear-factor.

Attire. Most conference attendees dress like corporate executives—navy suits, ties/scarves, dress shoes. For the presentation, you might want to wear something that draws attention away from your face. I have a problem watching people's faces during presentations because I tend to analyze facial expressions more than I analyze what's being said. I went to a panel where one of the speakers was wearing a large gold brooch. It mesmerized me, and I stayed focused on it for the entire presentation. But I also remember her talk very well.

You may want to consider the same thing, wearing an interesting tie or brooch as a focal point for your audience. Watching a nervous face is torture for the audience—it's difficult for people to listen when they're reacting to your discomfort. If you know they're focused on something else, you may be less nervous.

Visual aids. Slides or handouts are a great relief both to you and the audience. I've thought about (but haven't yet tried) preparing a handout of quotations from my paper so I could refer my audience to passages rather than reading them aloud. I think it would give the audience something concrete to ponder while they're listening to my argument. For other fields, slides may be a great way to focus your argument and prove your points graphically. You won't have to spend as much time explaining your data narratively and can concentrate on your main points. Visual aids are also a great way to keep attention focused away from your face. Be sure to put your name on one of the slides or the handout so the audience will remember your name after the session is over.

Role-playing. The best advice I ever received about public speaking: "Pretend you're someone else who has more confidence. I pretend I'm a drag queen when I do a reading." This worked like a charm. I felt so relaxed during one talk I almost jumped up on the conference table and began singing, "Ain't no mountain high enough . . ." You may not want to play this particular role (although it comes highly recommended from yours truly), but stepping into someone's shoes and playing a character can be a lot of fun. My "drag persona" helps to put me at a distance from my audience—I'm so into my character I don't have time to worry about the audience reaction. I've received good feedback from my talks, so this approach seems to work for the audience, too.

The paper itself. Most word processors default to standard 12-point type. If you're trying to read 12-point Times Roman from a podium, even if it's double-spaced, you'll have trouble keeping your place. Print out your paper in 14-point type for easy reading. A friend of mine also underlines words in red that she wants to emphasize. You might have trouble concentrating when you're reading off the page, so a few cues will help you sound like you're talking rather than reading. (Hey, it works for news anchors!) And don't staple your paper—clip the pages together instead. As you're reading, slide each page to the left as you finish it, so you don't make noise or break the flow of your reading.

The Q&A. Don't be upset if you don't get many questions in the Q&A session. Many times a good paper will be so convincing that the audience has nothing to add to your argument. If you get positive feedback in the form of interested questions, be enthusiastic in your responses. Keep some notes on hand that address any

PET PEEVE

It seems that audiences the world over cringe when a speaker introduces a quote verbally—"Eliot says, quote, 'Genuine poetry can communicate before it is understood,' unquote"—or the speaker indicates a quote by curling his or her fingers. A simple pause will do, folks, or a shift in tone. Audiences will get the message without elaborate (and amateurish) signs.

foreseeable gaps in your argument, as well as references from other sources to back up your argument. Usually that's all you need.

You may get a problem professor or student in the audience who just wants to show off his or her expertise by criticizing your own ("the heckler"). Look earnest in answering criticisms, but get back to the main points of your argument as swiftly as possible. Try not to let this person have control of the floor. Usually a sympathetic member of the audience will intercede on your behalf to debate with the heckler one-on-one or address more relevant questions directly to you. Fortunately, such situations are infrequent, and the rest of the audience will always be on your side. They've no doubt been in your place before and are especially protective of grad students.

PUBLISHING

Although this is the highest measure of success for academics, you should know that publishing your research does not result in monetary rewards. Scholarly publishing is notorious for its abysmal pay scale. But it does have its compensations. The best reward is getting your work out to the academic community where it may be cited and reviewed favorably. In addition, it's crucial that you publish to get a good tenure-track job. And once you've got a job your continued publishing credentials will be the biggest factor in a tenure review.

WHEN TO START SUBMITTING

You should not have to be prompted by your adviser to start publishing your work. The sooner you learn the publishing process, the more time you have to get into print. Journal lag time can take as much as three years from submission to publication. With such a long turnaround time, it makes sense to begin as soon as possible. If you've waited more than two years before trying to publish your research, you're falling behind your peers. I started trying to publish in my first year of graduate school. By the time I was finished with my program, I had about four articles circulating through the publishing channels.

INSIDER'S GUIDE TO JOURNAL PUBLISHING

Because I've worked for academic publications, I can give you some tips from the inside on successful publishing strategies.

Finding the appropriate journal. The quickest way to find the right journal is to consult a guide to all of the journals in your field. English scholars refer to the *MLA Directory of Periodicals*, which lists everything from circulation to submission requirements. Most fields have a similar kind of publication—just ask around. Once you have a list of possible journals compiled, go to the library and look at actual copies. Here are 10 factors to consider while you're browsing the journals.

1. Traditional or modern in appearance and content?
2. General or specific readership?
3. Editorial board: prestigious scholars or no-names?
4. Date of establishment: has it been around awhile?
5. Circulation: does it have a large readership?
6. Is it affiliated with an organization (and do you need to become a member before you can submit)?
7. Is it indexed in searchable databases?
8. Submission requirements: send "blind"? Do they want a query, abstract, or the finished article? What style guide do they use? How many copies do they want? What length do they request? Do they permit tables and illustrations? What format do they require for these?
9. Is the journal peer-reviewed? (More on this below.)
10. Articles: what is the length, tone, and style? How many notes? Trendy or traditional in content? Interdisciplinary?

REVIEW ISSUES OF THE JOURNAL

Yes, you should read the articles! Students desperate to publish have a bad habit of submitting to journals at which they've never even looked. If you do this you might as well save yourself some time and write your own rejection letter.

The mechanics of peer review. Most academic journals are peer-reviewed (these are also called "refereed" or "juried" journals). This means that the editor does not review your article, but forwards it to one or two scholars more familiar with your topic. These scholars review your article and decide whether or not it is publishable. Peer review helps assure that your article is judged competently and fairly by an expert.

Peer review is commonly "blind" or "double-blind." Journals that specify blind peer review request that you do not put your name anywhere in the article. You will of course have a cover letter with your name on it, which the editor places in a file. The editorial board consists of either the journal's core readers or scholars who recommend qualified readers to the editor. Blind review means that the readers don't know who you are, but you may know who they are. In double-blind submissions, you don't know the readers and they don't know you.

What's the holdup? You may be wondering why it takes so long to publish a scholarly article. Here's the answer: These outside readers and editorial board members are almost never paid. It's pro bono work for scholars, who generally list their editorial board experience in the "Service" section of the CV. Editors can't really pressure these readers to return an article. If they push readers too far by bugging them about deadlines, the reader may say, "Hey, I don't have time for this—find someone else." Editors dread hearing this! Readers may also be hard to find, especially if the topic area is very specialized. Thus, some readers will serve on several journals, adding to the time it takes for them to review articles.

Then there's the staffing shortage. As anyone knows, journal publishing is not a lucrative business. Unlike *Newsweek*, an academic journal staff usually consists of only a single editor, a business manager, and a couple of part-time grad students to handle production and proofing. And these overworked folks are processing hundreds of submissions a year. This takes time and adds to the publication delay.

Why multiple submissions are not OK. Some students, frustrated with the lag time for journal publication, want to submit an article to several journals. The norm for most journals is to forbid multiple submissions. If they allow it, they will say so in the submission requirements.

If, in spite of a policy against multiple submission, you choose to submit an article to more than one publication, you should be aware of the consequences. Remember, for a specialized topic, there may be only a few qualified readers, who probably review articles for more than one journal. If they read identical articles for different publications, have no doubt that they will report you to the editors! There's no better way to kill your publishing career before it even gets started. It annoys the readers and the editors, who are both overworked as it is. If you're fretting about getting published before you go gray, just remember that the lag time is no shorter for anyone else. No one's beating you to the punch.

The reader's report. Okay, so academic publishing takes forever and you don't get paid. But there's one tremendous advantage to academic publishing over commercial publishing: the reader's report. In most cases, even when your article is rejected, you will receive a one- to two-page report about it. The report will list both the strong and weak points of your article and may suggest that you make certain changes and try again for publication. I've seen readers' reports that even comment on grammar and sentence structure.

There is no more valuable tool for the novice academic writer than these reports. You're getting advice from the best scholars in the field. Your report may suggest other sources for you to look at, ways to improve your argument, and problems you need to address that you hadn't thought of before. It's essentially like having several editors. This specialized attention to your article provides the best advice you can get on improving your chances for future publication.

"R&R." A reader's report or letter from the editor that suggests you "revise and resubmit" is as good as getting published. Don't think of an R&R as a rejection—it's not. Take the reader's suggestions to heart, rewrite your article, and send it back within a couple of weeks. Most likely you'll hear from the editor with the good news that he or she is going to publish your article!

SHOULD YOU CALL THE EDITOR TO CHECK ON YOUR STATUS?

Most students are afraid of getting a rejection over the phone and will wait to get a reply by mail. Even though the journal submission turnaround time is protracted, you still have the right to professional courtesy.

If you don't get a response within the time specified in the submission guidelines, you're perfectly at liberty to call and check on the status of your manuscript. Editors get calls all the time.

If no response time is specified for a journal, I would suggest waiting two to three months before calling. After that, call and don't give up until you've tracked down the editor and gotten some kind of answer. If your article has been out for review for too long, a call could be the incentive an editor needs to contact a reader and get the report.

Rejection and what it means. So you get a rejection with a scathing reader's report. Do you drop your article into the "Later" folder? Absolutely not. You send it back out to the next journal. I probably shouldn't say this as an insider in this business, but the review process can seem incredibly arbitrary at times. It's a very subjective process because there are very subjective people involved, all with a variety of attitudes, writing styles, and political/critical orientations. An article that your first reader detests may be lauded by the next one.

I submitted an article based on a class paper I had written in my first quarter of grad school. A year and half later, with more experience in the field, I changed my mind completely about my argument. In fact, I disagreed with everything I had written and assumed any editor would see my article the same way. The article was ultimately rejected, but the last journal to review it told me that they had come very close to publishing it. The editor said it had sparked "considerable debate" among its readers, adding that the delay in notifying me was due to the length of time the readers spent discussing my essay.

I took this as encouraging news, and realized that one rejection does not necessitate rejection everywhere. The argument had been well written—good lead, an interesting and controversial subject, excellent support. All of these factors contributed to my article receiving serious consideration, even despite my own disagreement with its thesis!

Rewrite before resubmitting? One professor told me that his submission tactic was to send an article out to three journals successively before making any substantial rewrites. This may sound like he was ignoring the readers' reports, but he recognized the subjectivity of the review process. He stood by his work until he had racked up enough reports to compare them. Once he could see crossover criticisms from the reports, he edited the article substantially and sent it out again.

If you're skeptical about your first readers' reports, you may want to send your article to at least one more journal for review before making any substantial changes. It does save time. On the other hand, if you get advice on weaknesses in your argument that makes sense, go ahead and spend a week reworking your essay. Then get it back in the pipeline.

Top-down or bottom-up? The two theories of submissions: send it to the best journal first or start small and work your way up. I choose the former. Knowing that reviewers are people, not machines, I believe I should work my way down the prestige ladder. Who knows? I may get a favorable response from the best journal in the field before I've spent all that time submitting elsewhere.

Another reason to go for the top is to get a reader's report from the most recognized scholars in the field. Starting with a large circulation journal assures that you will receive the opinions of the experts about your topic. These scholars know (and write on) the current debates and usually provide valuable information and sources you may not get from less prominent readers.

The flip side of this argument is also convincing. If you want to get published quickly, you may not care where your article goes, as long as it goes to press. You can build a publishing reputation sooner, and one publication, even from a less prestigious journal, will give you credibility when you begin submitting elsewhere.

FROM PAPER OR THESIS/DISSERTATION CHAPTER TO ARTICLE

Turning a class paper or thesis/dissertation chapter into an article is a different process than adapting it for a conference. The only similarity is that they both require changing the tone of your paper. As with a conference paper, an article should have more of your own authoritative "voice" than a class paper. You want to assume a scholarly persona in your writing that is assertive but not arrogant. Use active rather than passive voice so you don't sound like you're hedging. If you're unsure about how to adopt this style, jot down words, common phrases, and organizational elements

GRAD STUDENT JOURNALS

Most fields have journals run by and for grad students. One avenue for quick publication might be to start with a graduate-level journal and work your way up the publication ladder.

HOW MUCH IS TOO MUCH?

Theses and dissertations are chock-full of exhaustive support and references. That's what you're trained to do.

For an article, however, you don't need to document every sentence. Assuming a voice of authority also means that you don't have to back up every single point in your argument. The YOU of the article needs to come through, and burying your voice under a pile of citations will distract from the narrative flow of your "story."

The easiest way to learn how to do this is to read articles in the journal to which you're submitting. Follow the same formula for your references and you'll better your chances at publication.

you've liked in other scholarly articles. When you get stuck with your revisions, refer to this "cheat sheet" for inspiration. Here are a few other tips:

Technical sophistication. Conference papers, as I suggested, should keep technical language to a minimum for easier reading and comprehension. Articles for publication, however, demand a higher level of what I call "field terminology." I'm not advocating the use of jargon (although published articles seem rife with it), but you should use a level of technical sophistication that matches your specialized readership. And remember that this level may vary from journal to journal.

Longer sentences are OK. In academic prose I tend to write longish sentences, almost against my will. Perhaps subconsciously I'm mimicking the writing style of all of the literature I've read during my research. It's always a good idea to say what you want as succinctly as possible, but academics expect complex sentence structure. Use your own judgment. Because you're not preparing the article as a speech, you have more flexibility with syntax and length. And, because you'll be incorporating more technical or critical language in an article, your sentences may need to be longer to express a single idea.

Start with a good lead. Your first paragraph should be an overview of what you're covering in the full article, but that doesn't mean it has to be formulaic. Try to catch the reader's attention with an engaging lead-in. If your article draws a startling conclusion, say so up front. With all the competition out there in the publishing arena, it makes sense to write something that stands out from the stack of submissions. Be a little creative, maybe break a few college essay-writing rules, and try to open with a bang.

Present solid documentation and support. Unlike the conference paper, which should concentrate on your ideas rather than on supporting sources, the published article always includes plenty of supporting references. It's easy to understand why: no one wants to be accused of plagiarizing someone else's work.

An article usually includes endnotes that cite sources tangentially related to the topic at hand. How many times have you seen an endnote that says, "For more on this topic, see X's article . . ."? I used to abhor these kinds of endnotes (if the source doesn't contribute directly to the discussion, why include it in the first place?), but now I recognize that the author is demonstrating his or her general knowledge of the field as well as the specific topic. And occasionally I've used these related sources in my own research. Don't be afraid to use endnotes liberally in your revision. Show off your reading!

Adapt your format. This is one of the biggest problems for students submitting work for publication. One journal may specify "Chicago" and another "APA." Or a journal may use a combination of formats and mail out guidelines with specifics. Students are notorious for ignoring these guidelines. Know what happens if you neglect this seemingly trivial requirement? You get your article back unread.

During the submissions process, you will no doubt end up with several versions of your article—one that uses footnotes, one that uses endnotes, one in which references are incorporated into your text, and another in which references are placed in a bibliography. But it's imperative that each article you send out conforms to the journal's submission requirements. Yes, it takes time, and yes, it's grunt work. But it matters more than you think. Good presentation can positively influence your readers.

OTHER PUBLISHING OPPORTUNITIES

While the academic article is the standard form of research publication, there are plenty of other avenues for breaking into publishing. Here are a few suggestions for getting into other kinds of print sources.

BOOK REVIEWS

I've been told by one professor that a book review doesn't count much in the overall "Publishing" section

In such a competitive job market, students are now trying to get the dissertation published as soon as it's completed to improve their employment prospects. If your professors are telling you not to worry about this right now, ignore them. The job climate has changed dramatically since they were in grad school. You need every edge you can get!

of the CV. However, I think doing book reviews is a great way to network from the inside of the publishing arena. Book reviews also give you a chance to publish early in your program before you've had time to put together a full-blown article. You can approach doing book reviews two ways. If a new book that you want to review comes on the market, you can contact the book review editors of several journals and ask if they'd be interested in having it reviewed. The other method is to contact a book review editor first, tell him or her your area of specialization, and offer your services as a reviewer.

Book reviews are formulaic, and the formula is easy to adapt. Just take a look at sample published reviews, and you'll see the pattern. A review usually covers the book chapters in order, over several paragraphs. The last paragraph discusses any weaknesses in the argument and balances those weaknesses against the book's overall quality. A bad book does not get reviewed, by the way. It's unprofessional to slam a colleague's book in print, and it doesn't help anyone's research to use a poorly written or argued text. If you begin reading a book for a review and see that it has serious problems, stop reading. There's no point in spending more time on it. Just let the editor know and you'll get another assignment.

PUBLISHING THROUGH A UNIVERSITY PRESS

In most cases, the only book-length work you'll have the opportunity to publish as a student is your dissertation. And you probably won't get around to revising your dissertation while you're still in school. Most guides on publishing dissertations recommend that you let the completed dissertation sit around for a year or so before revising it.

Below are a few suggestions for revising your work and approaching a book publisher.

Dreaded "dissertationese." Most university press editors can spot an unrevised dissertation in a New York minute. Common elements of "dissertationese" include defensive writing, in which the narrative flow is broken by constant appeals to the literature, being apologetic for material not covered, and constant repetition of points in the argument. In general, dissertations are on specific, narrowly focused subjects. All of these elements suggest that the dissertation needs to be substantially revised before it's ready for publication. The only way to do this with confidence is to read some of the books published by prospective presses. This will take some time, but it will also help you target the best presses for your research.

Different audience. Typically, a book audience is much more general than your dissertation audience. In the dissertation chapter, I said that you should customize your writing style for your audience, i.e., your dissertation committee. Though this is good advice for speeding you out of grad school, it will add time to the revising you'll do later when you want to publish your research. Your dissertation will probably have to be altered if it's going to be of interest to a more general audience. For publication, you will probably have to expand your topic area, and this kind of revision will most likely entail more research. Large portions of your dissertation may need to be cut entirely.

The unsolicited manuscript no-no. How many unsolicited manuscripts get published? According to a recent survey of 74 university press editors, only 2 percent. Yes, you read it correctly! The standard format for submitting your book to a university press is a query. A query includes a cover letter, a sample table of contents or outline, and a sample chapter or chapters (usually the first one or two chapters of your book). In the cover letter you should usually state, in order, the following information:

- Subject of the book, anticipated page length, and positive feedback you've already received (for example, name-drop prestigious colleagues who have read your manuscript and recommended that you publish it)
- Competition (other books published on this topic or, even better, lack of competition)
- Intended audience
- Your qualifications

All of this information should fit on one page if possible. Make sure in your cover letter to address the editor by name. There are plenty of sources that will list the current university press editor; don't send a form letter. Most editors claim that they send responses back within two weeks of receiving a query. Color me skeptical, but this sounds rather optimistic. If you don't hear back from an editor within a month or so, call and find out the status of your query.

Multiple submissions. According to a recent survey, 37 percent of university presses allow multiple submissions. If you decide to submit to several editors, be sure to specify in your cover letter that you're submitting to more than one publisher—you can even list the others you're considering. These editors won't mind a multiple submission, but they want to know about it when they get your proposal.

Peer review. Like academic journals, university press editors typically use outside readers to evaluate your work, although editors review all queries. If an editor expresses interest in your full manuscript, you should know that he or she will then farm out your manuscript to another scholar (usually two) who will read and recommend or reject your manuscript. This process is time-consuming, just as it is for journal peer review. Still, you should contact the editor if you do not get a response back within a few months. Most editors respect authors who want to know what's going on with their manuscripts. It's good business practice and not unprofessional.

Contract. If your manuscript is accepted, you will receive a standard contract from the publisher outlining both your rights and the rights of the publisher. If you're new to contract negotiations, several good sources offer tips on getting the most out of the contract. Don't go into contract negotiations without doing a little research first. The terms written into the contract are not written in stone. They're often just a starting point for negotiations between the author and the publisher. Negotiation should be handled professionally and amicably; it's not an adversarial contest. At the same time, however, you want to get a good royalty and advance agreement (some of these academic books do make money), and retain as many rights as you can. Check the annotated bibliography for more on successful contract negotiations.

ELECTRONIC PUBLISHING

Despite the apocalyptic predictions of many journal editors that electronic publishing would replace print journals, it doesn't look like the traditional journal is being abolished just yet. Many scholars continue to tell their students that publishing in an on-line journal is not a "real" publication. As long as they continue to have this bias, print publication will remain the primary objective for students interviewing for academic jobs.

But grad students recognize, more than the older generation of scholars, that electronic publishing has obvious advantages over print publication. The lag time for on-line journals is substantially shorter than traditional academic journals. Scientific journals are moving ahead electronically for just this reason. Scientific research needs to get out in the field as soon as possible. Intense competition in the sciences necessitates fast publication of results.

But if you choose to pursue electronic publishing, be aware that copyright issues for on-line journals are still a gray area. The wording of the 1976 Copyright Act protects work as soon as it's created, rather than when it's published, so it would seem that your work is safe whether it ends up on-line or in print. In practice, however, the legal issues of electronic publishing are still being worked out. If you pursue this option, make sure the on-line journal to which you submit has a clearly worded statement about copyright, fair use, and reprint rights. A good on-line journal will make an effort to address these issues responsibly.

CHAPTER

GETTING A JOB

My job search strategies? Hmm. Voodoo? Oneiromancy? Terrorist threats? "DeAR proFeSSOr johNSOn: iF yOu EvEr wANt tO sEe yOur beLOVed pOOdLe aLivE AgaIn, hIRe ME iMMedIAteLY . . ."

—Kelli, Ph.D. student, English

Despite the fact that the job search is the final stage of grad school, job search strategies should be an ongoing component of your work. From classes to conferences to publishing, you should be involved in making contacts and evaluating research that will appeal to potential employers. The job search doesn't begin when the thesis/dissertation is finished. It begins the moment you start choosing a graduate program.

And here, at the end of the book, I must impart some bleak news. If you've been keeping up with *The Chronicle of Higher Education*, you know that the academic market is changing—dramatically and for the worse. In my field, schools receive an average of 300 applications for a single tenure-track position. At very prestigious research universities, the applications can top out at around 800. English is one of the worst fields, but the news is not good anywhere in the arts and sciences. One science student at a top-ten university says that his department produces 50 Ph.D.s a year but only hires two new professors. You do the math.

"IT'S THE ECONOMY, STUPID"

So what's going on? What about that job boom that everyone predicted for the 1990s? That prediction was based on the expectation that older professors would begin retiring, making way for younger scholars in the job market. Some schools, however, have eliminated their mandatory retirement age policies, so those tenured professors are staying put. Other universities have offered early retirement incentives to tenured professors. While that sounds like good news to the job seeker, these universities are not replacing their tenured professors with tenure-track assistant professors. Instead, the university has replaced them with short-term appointments, adjunct faculty, and more grad student TA's. Cary Nelson, professor at the University of Illinois and an outspoken critic of the state of academia, states that 40 percent of all faculty members in higher education are part-timers.

THE NONACADEMIC JOB SEARCH

Why did I put this section before the academic job search? Because I believe it's the best way to go for employment right now, particularly for the humanities grad student. You should be spending most of your effort on targeting nonacademic employers.

PROS OF NONACADEMIC EMPLOYMENT

A nonacademic job search will usually take several months to a year. This may sound like a long time until you consider the academic alternative. We've all heard stories of Ph.D.s going on job search rounds for two years or more, taking a short-term appointment or post-doc and interviewing year after year for a permanent job. Ph.D.s who stay on the job circuit for more

LABOR CUTBACKS

The downsizing model that corporations employed during the 1980s has filtered down to universities as well, as they receive less government funding and look for ways to cut costs. Not surprisingly, cutting labor costs comes first.

Networking was my key to getting a job offer. I was offered a post-doc after giving a talk! The more contacts you have, the better your chances. Post-docs are always in demand, but if you have a good adviser, he or she can get you places.
—*Arthur, Ph.D. student, Psychology*

than a year also have ever-growing competition—every year a new crop of Ph.D.s is added to the pool of candidates.

And speaking of rewards. . . . This may be a new concept to grad students: outside academe, time equals money! Your time suddenly takes on value, especially if you pursue self-employment and independent consulting. Every hour you work translates into dollars. After spending three months writing an article and only getting a few copies of a journal as compensation, an hourly wage can be a refreshing change.

Students with advanced degrees are attractive to employers outside of academe. You're the intellectual cream of the crop outside the Ivory Tower, regardless of the subject of your dissertation or your field of specialization. Employers weigh the Ph.D. as a credential in itself, without evaluating your dissertation's content or marketability. In some fields, especially consulting firms, each degree you hold will bump up your salary grade, regardless of the subject you studied. In addition, nonacademic employers know they can train you with little effort. You're bright and won't need a lot of hand-holding. This saves employers money, which is always a primary concern.

GETTING STARTED

Hey, this doesn't sound like a bad idea! But without established networks or guidelines for a nonacademic job search, you may not know how to begin. Do you know what it takes to get a nonacademic job? Research. What could be easier after years of training in research techniques?

SKILLS INVENTORY: PROCESS, NOT PRODUCT

Nonacademic employers, unlike their academic counterparts, are not as interested in the products of your graduate work. They're interested more in skills than publication credits. You have to start by rethinking the whole idea of credentials. Take a look at the things you can do that might be valuable to an industry employer. And, believe me, you have several skills. A sample skills inventory would look something like this:

- Teaching/training
- Writing and publishing
- Conducting and organizing research
- Performing experiments
- Public speaking
- Managing subjects/animals
- Administrative skills (committee duties, grade tracking, memos, and reports)
- Service (student groups, research assistantships)
- Electronic skills (technology in the classroom, on-line research)
- Programming
- Statistical analysis
- Grantsmanship

Not a bad start for a list of transferrable skills. You also have an ability, much valued in a nonacademic job market, to juggle several projects at once—teaching, administration, publishing, writing grants, and so on. Nonacademic employers are often concerned that grad students, withdrawn from the "real world," cannot adapt to a dynamically changing environment. But grad students, perhaps more so than folks outside of academe, do just that. The demands of grad school require a student to be flexible. Stress your adaptability to potential employers, who may have a misconception that the academy involves only cloistered research.

In addition, your ability to communicate effectively in the classroom, at conferences, or on paper will set you apart from competing MBAs who are mostly trained in technical aspects of business. Not only do you have solid analytical skills and flexibility, but also the ability to make sense of data/research and present it to others. And you have a good deal of experience working with people—managing students, mediating conflicts, and solving problems.

TRANSFERABLE SKILLS

Don't worry if your research into Florentine architecture doesn't seem very useful to an advertising agency. Remember, employers are interested in your range of process skills. Through your published articles and conference presentations you have gained valuable—and transferable—expertise.

POTENTIAL INDUSTRIES

Know where students with advanced degrees go? Here's a small sample of the fields they work in:

- accounting
- advertising
- analysis—legislative, investment, financial, policy
- banking
- commercial technology
- communications
- computer software and hardware development
- consumer products
- corporate educational consulting
- state, local, and national government—NEH, NEA, NIMH, NIH, NSF, USIA, Dept. of Education, Dept. of State, Dept. of Defense, even the CIA!
- human resources
- insurance
- libraries
- management consulting
- museums and art councils
- public affairs and public relations
- publishing
- retail
- research and development
- teaching abroad
- writing—screenwriter, education writer, columnist, corporate PR, technical writing, freelance

FINDING AN INDUSTRY (OR, SKIP THE WANT ADS)

The point of a skills inventory is for you to find an industry to target rather than the other way around. Don't peruse the job ads looking for something targeted to people with advanced degrees. It's a waste of time. You've probably heard that the good jobs never get advertised—that's absolutely true. The high-level professional jobs you're seeking are almost always filled through personal contacts.

When you have a list of skills, start thinking about what you'd like to do for a living. You can probably work in just about any industry, so don't assume you're limited to jobs related to your field. There are humanities scholars who go into investment analysis and scientists who write successful novels. Your university's career counseling center probably offers vocational testing, such as the popular Strong-Campbell test, which can give you an idea of the kinds of occupations that match your interests and personality. (Let's hope there's not a category for "Perennial Grad Student"!)

ON-LINE AND LIBRARY RESOURCES

Once you have an idea of fields of interest, start doing research. You've got it easier than your counterparts in the 1980s because of—you guessed it!—the World Wide Web. There are several Web sites devoted to academics looking for jobs in a nonacademic environment. You will start to get an idea of those industries that are most interested in hiring people with advanced degrees. These on-line resources may let you know of new jobs before they get into print.

JOB SEARCHING ON THE WEB

Here are three great on-line resources for finding both academic and nonacademic jobs:

- Jobtrack (http://www.jobtrak.com/jobguide). Rated top 5 percent by Point Survey, this comprehensive job site lists both academic and nonacademic jobs. It's the best resource for grad students seeking jobs outside the university environment. It covers all fields and all job opportunities, including government jobs. Jobtrack also has helpful links to other Web sites including "Career Planning," "Internships and Summer Work," and "Research Resources," which can help you find information on specific companies and/or cities you're considering.
- Academe This Week (http://chronicle.merit.edu/.ads/.links.html). This job source is compiled from *The Chronicle of Higher Education* job listings. It covers all disciplines. Although it stresses academic and administrative positions within the university, it includes listings for nonacademic jobs as well. You can do a search by region, including international job listings.
- Academic Positions Network (gopher://wcni.cis.umn.edu:11111/1). This gopher site lists academic and nonacademic jobs, including international job opportunities. Covers all disciplines and includes a searchable index.

Doing subject searches on the Web is also a great way to locate companies. Check different companies' Web sites and read their press releases, annual reports, company bios—anything and everything. Make a list of names of company officers you might want to contact. See where company offices are located and if there are offices overseas. Also, use the library to supplement your search. The library may contain copies of annual reports, 10Ks, quarterly earnings reports, and articles on the company that you can track down in newspaper indexes.

The library will also have trade publications that can help you narrow your search from a broad field to specific companies. Browsing these magazines, you will find out about new technologies and trends in the industry and who's setting the standards. Trade publications also include want ads, so you can get an idea of the kinds of jobs available and the credentials for which employers are looking. You shouldn't even begin to work

Many students in my field get post-docs by contacting a researcher prior to finishing the dissertation and suggesting a collaboration. The post-doc may then be funded by a grant (sometimes written by both parties), or by a pool of funds from the institution. Science *magazine is probably the most common source for finding jobs in my field.*

—Jenny, Ph.D. student, Biology

If you can't find a university internship program or partnership that fits your interest, consider working a few hours a week in a company for free. You're used to working without pay by now, but this time your efforts may be rewarded—and quickly—with a real wage.

I wish incoming students were given clear, brutally clear, statistics about jobs. Students should look at the CVs of those who have managed to get jobs so they will know what it takes to make it.
—*Kathy, Ph.D. student, History of Science*

on your résumé until you've looked at some of the qualifications and background requirements in the want ads.

TAKING OUTSIDE CLASSES

Once you begin narrowing the job search, you'll see how your qualifications fit with different industries. You may want to supplement your departmental course work with classes that might enhance your nonacademic qualifications. This is one of the reasons I say that the job search should begin early in your graduate career. Adapting your skills to nonacademic as well as academic employers takes time. Common supplemental course work includes computer programming, statistics, intro economics (macro and micro), intro business classes (accounting, finance, management), and technology classes (Internet, Web, technology in the classroom, distance learning, and so on). If you've targeted a specific industry, like film screenwriting, then you can take a class or two in the film department.

INTERNSHIPS

Practical experience may be your best bet in landing a nonacademic job. Summer jobs, internships, co-op programs, and similar opportunities can give you hands-on experience and tell you whether or not an industry is for you. It's also a great way to network. I heard one story of a Ph.D. grad donating her time to an organization and getting a full-time job offer within a matter of weeks.

NETWORKING

Many universities have partnerships with outside companies, offering students the opportunity to get some part-time work experience and meet people in a variety of jobs. Unfortunately for humanities students, these excellent networking opportunities are well established only in the sciences and social sciences. Because humanities students are being trained for academic life, your department and university will not have contacts or networks for humanities-related jobs outside of academe. You've got to do the networking on your own.

Career counseling. When you were in college, you were no doubt encouraged to use the career counseling center to find alumni working in your fields of interest. You still have this option, even as a grad student. Find alumni (and grad students, if the center maintains information on them) who are working in companies or industries that appeal to you. And don't forget about the career counseling center at your undergrad institution. You probably still have privileges there as an alum yourself, although some centers charge a fee for alumni networking services.

Department placement record. Your department maintains records of the job placement of its graduates. Given the state of the academic job market, many of them will be working in nonacademic jobs. If you want to work in a nonacademic field, approach the departmental secretary and get information about where former grad students are working.

Grad students in other fields. If you're a humanities student looking to break into a scientific field, it may be time to meet some science or computer science grad students. Part of my English specialty includes a related interest in electronic publishing. I have already begun networking with computer science students about job opportunities related to on-line technology. They tell me about new trends in on-line research, forward interdisciplinary Calls for Papers, and suggest good companies for a future job search.

For humanities grads looking for internship or summer employment in their own fields, you may be able to tap into existing science and social science job networks by making contact with some of those grad students. They can tell you about their own experiences interning for different employers. They can also point you to professors who have contacts at several

USE UNDERGRAD JOB RESOURCES

Career counseling centers typically offer seminars for undergrad students about getting jobs. You can attend these seminars and workshops, too. And why not attend university job fairs? Talking with a rep from a company in your area of interest may be a valuable contact. Even though the rep may be looking for college grads with accounting degrees, he or she can give you names of company employees doing the same kind of work you want to do.

STEPS TO NETWORKING

Remember that a scientific research company probably hires marketing people, technical writers, public affairs coordinators, and so on. A company that has a long-standing relationship with the university's scientific community may also be a great place for a humanities student to find a job. These companies already hire science grad students; they may be willing to hire grad students in other fields from the same university.

Example: Say you're a philosophy student who's interested in making a change to corporate communications. Talking with grad students and professors in the sciences will be a first step in getting the names of companies that collaborate with the university. The science professor can give you the name of the R&D director, and the R&D director can give you the name of the marketing director. You've got your foot in the door. It's that easy.

companies or government agencies. You've got a valuable information source right in your own university. And wouldn't it be great to meet some grad students outside your own field?

Crossover conferences. If you're targeting employment prospects related to your academic field, find conferences that cover business issues rather than academic ones, or interdisciplinary conferences that blend academic and nonacademic topics. These kinds of conferences are rare in academe, but if you can find one, you'll get a chance to make contacts with nonacademic employers who take an interest in us "academic types."

If you're moving out of your field entirely, you may want to attend an academic conference in the field into which you would like to move. Professors would be interested to meet a student from one field who's considering employment in another and wants to know about job opportunities. And they'll appreciate your level of commitment in attending a conference just to get more information. A professor in psychology has probably never run into a history grad student at a conference!

Former/current employers, friends, and family. You may have a bill-paying job that could turn into a more challenging job opportunity once you've graduated. Or you may have had a previous job in a field you'd like to work in again. It's no secret that office workers enjoy chatting during the long hours of the work day. Talk to employees about the kinds of work their friends and family do. This is a great source of networking for finding people doing all kinds of work.

NEXT STOP: INFORMATIONAL INTERVIEW

Once you've compiled a list of companies that interest you, you'll need to find a way into them. Fortunately, we have the 1980s to thank for introducing a creative and low-stress approach to job hunting: the informational interview. It's a great way to get information about a company without the mental agony of an out-and-out job interview.

Call and ask if you can schedule 20 minutes to meet with your contact to learn more about his or her job and the company. Mention the name of the person who referred you. Say that you're considering job fields outside academe and want to know more about the nuts and bolts of his or her work. Most people are happy to talk about themselves, and a little flattery can go a long way in this initial contact. You might mention something like, "I saw your bio on the company's Web page and was interested to hear more about your role in X—it sounds like a fascinating project." Or, "I've been doing some background research on the company, and your name keeps coming up. I thought you'd be the best person to talk to about company operations."

I don't need to tell you to dress appropriately for an informational interview. You should treat this interview like it is the real thing. It's better to dress more stylishly than you would for an academic conference. A dash of color in a tie or scarf makes a cosmopolitan impression. A good rule of thumb when you're shopping is to find business attire that's one rung down from the most expensive clothing in the store. It's ironic but true that in order to get a job you have to look like you don't need one.

WHAT YOU'LL ASK THEM

Some employees may jump right into an informational interview during an initial phone contact. It's important to be prepared. Here are a few questions you might want to ask:

- What is your background and education?
- Were you promoted to this position or hired from outside?
- Can you tell me more about your work in the area of . . .?
- How does your job integrate with the rest of your department/company?
- Is your department expanding?
- What are the possibilities for advancement in your department? In your position?

CIRCUMVENT HUMAN RESOURCES

Human resources people are not really trained to hire new employees, despite what you may think. Their job is to handle the bureaucratic administrative details of hiring—placing ads, culling resumes, following through on EEO procedures, scheduling interviews. Managers, directors, VPs, and other company executives actually conduct the interviews and make the final decisions. Find these "power brokers" when you're ready to do informational interviews.

DON'T DO ALL THE TALKING

It's an interesting facet of human nature that the less you talk, the more intelligent you appear to others. Good listening skills are at least as important as good conversation skills. Listening to an employer, really listening, gives you time to think about responses and come up with perceptive questions in return. It will also keep you from blurting out something incoherent or deranged under stress. Remember the three C's of interviewing: calm, cool, and collected.

- What do you think will be the future of this business? What skills will be the most valuable?
- Is there a lot of competition for people who want to pursue this career?
- What is a typical "day in the life" for you?
- What duties are covered in your job description?

WHAT THEY'LL ASK YOU

Whether this is an informational interview or the real thing, company executives tend to ask the same questions to people with advanced degrees. Here are a few, adapted from Groneman and Lear's *Corporate Ph.D.: Making the Grade in Business*:

- Why did you pursue a degree in such a narrow field?
- Can you meet deadlines and produce results quickly?
- Can you work with a team, or are you more comfortable working alone or with other academics?
- Are you flexible enough to work in a rapidly changing environment?
- Do you get bored with day-to-day administrative details?
- Can you accept that you won't own your work in this business?
- Would you leave if you were offered an academic position?
- Do you consider yourself aggressive and/or competitive?
- What kinds of skills do you have to offer this company/job?
- Do you have any related experience?
- What are your long-range career plans?

You can see from these questions that corporate executives are primarily concerned with your ability to adapt and grow in a dynamic environment. It's your job to demonstrate to them that your academic experience mirrors in many ways a corporate structure. If you can show executives that academe involves collaboration, deadlines, "real-world" work, competition, and administrative duties, you can dispel employers' misconceptions about academic life. This is also the time to mention outside job experiences like internships, course work related to business practices, and your "people skills"—teaching, counseling, and public speaking. Use your research to ask thoughtful questions and prove that you've done your homework on the company.

Once the interview is finished, pass along a copy of your résumé and ask that he or she keep you in mind if a position becomes available. Ask them for a few names of other people you should talk with to find out more about the business. Be sure to send a thank-you note that lets the person know you appreciate the time he or she spent talking with you, and that you're more interested than ever in this kind of job. Repeat your request to keep you in mind if a position becomes available.

IF YOU GET A JOB OFFER

Sometimes you may be offered a job on the spot. The informational interview can function the same as an interview for a job. Remember that you're talking to the folks who actually do the hiring. This cuts out the whole bureaucratic process. Many times you will be offered an entry-level position as a trial run, so your employer can see if you have what it takes to work in the company. Should you take it? My advice is a resounding YES! If you take a look at assistant professor salaries, you'll see that many corporate entry-level jobs actually pay as much or more money as a starting academic salary.

FOOLPROOF STRATEGY FOR LANDING A JOB

In doing your research, be thinking of ways that you could improve business operations. The single most successful approach to getting a job is to walk into an interview and solve a business problem the company didn't know it had. This requires a lot of research, both on the company and its competitors, but the payoff will make it worth it. If you can help to streamline an operation, or suggest technology or resources that can benefit the company, get ready to be offered a great job. This kind of company knowledge and motivation will impress an employer. Chances are you'll bypass the entry-level job offer altogether.

THE CORPORATE LADDER VS. THE IVORY TOWER

Unlike academe, where you spend many years proving yourself before you get promoted, corporate promotion is quick. And your pay level increases significantly with each move up the ladder. It's not uncommon to move up two rungs on the corporate ladder within only a couple of years. In business you are a resource, just as much as any other new product a company uses to get ahead. Company execs want to put you where you will benefit them the most. If you can handle more responsibility, it will be quickly offered.

THE ACADEMIC JOB SEARCH

Academic employment is a buyer's market right now, and it doesn't look as if the market will change anytime soon. Getting an academic job involves a serious time commitment. Not only that, it can involve a serious financial investment as well. Many organizations charge a substantial fee just to receive their published job listings! In addition, you'll spend money on everything from dossier services, transcript fees, copies, and mailing to travel expenses to attend conferences for the initial interview (yes, you pay for the first interview). If you're using the common "spray and pray" method of getting a job, which involves sending out as many as 100 application packets, you're looking at a serious depletion of dinero.

Another irony of the academic job search is the fact that, despite your training in specialized research, most academic employers are primarily interested in your teaching skills. Thus, the emphasis is not on your research credentials, a.k.a. your thesis/dissertation, but your general knowledge of the field and your teaching experience. Why? Because that's primarily what you'll be doing when you start out in a tenure-track or short-term appointment: teaching undergraduates.

FINDING JOBS

Aside from the on-line resources listed earlier, there are several print publications for academic job seekers. If you're interested in working in the university administration rather than going tenure-track in a specific department, academic job lists include these university positions as well. The most common printed resource for students in both the arts and sciences is *The Chronicle of Higher Education*. Students looking for specific jobs in their fields usually consult one or more of the following: *MLA Job List*, *Science*, *Affirmative Action Register*, *National Arts Job Bank*, *Community Jobs*, and the

Federal Jobs register. By the end of your first year in grad school you should know which publications and on-line sources are commonly used to find jobs in your field. Many fields have discussion groups dedicated to job postings (such as sci.research.careers, sci.research.postdoc, bio.jobs.offered, and so on). Don't wait until you've finished your thesis/dissertation to get familiar with these sources.

COVER LETTER

Keep your letter to a single page. The standard academic cover letter includes the following information, in order:

- Who you are
- Where you heard about the job (name-dropping is very common)
- Title of your thesis/dissertation
- Adviser's name
- Interest in teaching
- Teaching experience
- Related administrative or leadership positions
- Grants awarded
- List of enclosed materials (or "dossier enclosed")
- Request to discuss the position in an interview

INTERVIEWING ON A HOTEL BED

If you came to grad school from a corporate environment, the typical academic screening interview is going to seem a little bizarre. Most initial academic interviews are conducted at large national conferences rather than at the university, mainly as a way for the department to save time and money. A school will contact you by phone and schedule an interview sometime during the conference.

A WORD ABOUT "APPRENTICESHIP"

The sciences, more than other fields, take the apprentice model of graduate training seriously. In most cases, a science student's adviser is the key to getting published, landing jobs, post-doc opportunities, and networking outside the department. In the humanities, and to some extent the social sciences, students are less likely to build on or contribute directly to an adviser's work. As a result, an adviser has less impact on these students' academic job possibilities.

CAVEATS ABOUT ADJUNCTING

Most adjunct faculty are extremely dissatisfied with their positions. If you choose to go this route because tenure-track opportunities are scarce, you should be aware of the most common problems adjuncts face:

- Low pay for teaching lots of courses. Sometimes adjuncts teach as many as five classes per semester. Their pay may be only slightly higher than a TA's income.

- Inadequate job preparation. Adjuncts are typically expected to dive right into their teaching responsibilities. Sometimes this lack of preparation leads to bad teaching evaluations.

- Scapegoating. Tenured professors may blame poor teaching standards on adjunct faculty and student TA's.

- "Paying dues" philosophy. Students preparing for the job market may be told by senior faculty that adjuncting is a part of the dues a young scholar pays to land a permanent job.

- Out of the loop. Adjuncts are not students, nor are they full-time faculty members. They may be willfully or accidentally neglected by the department, thus cutting off valuable networking opportunities.

And it gets weirder. Most interviews take place in a hotel room. The committee may have arranged to have a suite for interviewing candidates, which means that you'll sit at a dining table with the rest of the faculty committee. But some schools cannot afford even this luxury, and you will be interviewed on a hotel bed with strangers. Be prepared to do your interview in a confined (and rather intimate) space!

Below is a list of the questions most commonly asked at interviews. Most of these questions are directed toward evaluating your teaching. It's important when you begin the academic job search to reorient your skills away from research and toward the classroom. Some of these questions are adapted from Anthony and Roe's *Finding a Job in Your Field*.

- Why did you go to grad school?
- Who has influenced you the most as a scholar?
- What are your long-range career plans?
- Why are you applying to our university?
- What is your style of teaching?
- What is the student composition of your classes (how many and diversity of students)?
- How did you decide on your thesis/dissertation topic?
- When will you finish your degree?
- What courses have you taught?
- Are you willing to teach in the summer?
- If you were to teach such-and-such a course, what texts and approach would you use and why?
- Is there anything in your background that will make a special contribution to this department?
- Tell me about your course work.
- How would you teach traditional vs. nontraditional students?
- What are your grading policies?
- What courses would you like to design?
- How will you balance your teaching and your research?
- How, if at all, does your dissertation research translate to the undergraduate classroom?

NO-NO QUESTIONS

Even though some questions are highly inappropriate (even illegal) during a screening interview, that doesn't mean faculty won't ask them, particularly to female candidates. Questions may include your marital status, plans for having a family, spouse's employment and willingness to relocate, religious affiliation or membership in political/social organizations, mental and physical health and history, even criminal record.

You can deflect these questions a couple of ways if you're not comfortable answering them. You can respond with, "Will this be evaluated as part of my qualifications for the position?" Or, "I am certain this will not be a problem, if that's what you're asking." I prefer a humorous approach to head off these kinds of personal questions. If they ask whether or not you're planning to have a family, you might say, "Hmm. I'm not sure—what's the right answer?" A little humor may steer them clear of personal questions without any awkwardness. Whatever approach you use, have a response prepared in advance so you're not caught off guard.

SECOND INTERVIEW: CAMPUS VISIT

If you get a call from a university after the conference or conference-call interview, get excited! Instead of a one-in-twenty shot at a job, your chances have usually been narrowed to one-in-three. The competition is more intense, but your chances are also much improved. You can use this scheduling call as an opportunity to ask some questions about your campus visit and interview. Here are some questions, both logistical and substantive, that you should ask about the campus interview, adapted from Anthony and Roe's *Finding a Job in Your Field*.

- What is the agenda for my visit?
- Will I be expected to prepare a lecture or teach a class?
- If I do a lecture, who will be my audience (students, faculty, both)?
- Will there be a reception with the faculty?

PHONE INTERVIEW

It's becoming more common for faculty to schedule a conference call interview. Sure, you save traveling expenses, but all of the students I know who did this found it agonizing.

Without important visual cues, it can be difficult to interpret tone of voice and the meaning of "the question behind the question." Also, conference calls are full of awkward pauses. No one—particularly not the candidate!—wants to speak over the top of someone else. There may be no way out of a conference call, so be prepared for these differences.

The good thing about doing an interview over the phone is that you have your notes on hand—you can write down and read your responses if you get stuck. You can even dress in your pajamas if it helps you relax. Who's going to know?

OFFER SAMPLE SYLLABI

You can make a fabulous impression on the faculty committee by offering sample syllabi of a couple of the department's undergraduate classes. Before your visit, take a look at the department's undergraduate course listings to find out what courses are offered regularly. See what texts and approaches are used. Then draft a syllabus or two of the same classes that includes your own choices of texts and exercises.

PREPARING A TALK

Know your audience before you prepare a lecture. If you can find out from the school beforehand what kinds of subjects they want you to cover, so much the better. Many schools, however, will not have a topic specified, and candidates will usually address some aspect of their dissertation.

If you do this, keep your talk general enough so that grad students outside your area of specialization can understand it. And keep it within the time limit specified—the shorter the better. Prepare a handout with your name on it so people will remember who you are.

And, if you talk about your dissertation, expect to get questions about how your research will contribute to the undergraduate classroom.

- Will I be meeting with graduate students as well as faculty?
- Can I arrange a tour of the city with a faculty member during my stay?
- Will I be picked up at the airport?
- Are my expenses covered for the visit?

MORE RESEARCH

If you haven't done research already to prepare for your first interview, now is the time to learn all you can about the faculty and school. This involves the usual information gathering—faculty publications, department/university promotional materials, and finding out if any professors in your own department know faculty at the school where you'll be interviewing. As always, name-dropping is an important way to break the ice. You should also check out starting salaries for assistant professors at that university using the Faculty Salaries Database, available on the Web at http://tikkun.ed.asu.edu/aaup. The database is compiled by the American Association of University Professors and includes just about every university in the country. You can even do comparative analyses between schools. You may not be asked about salary during the interview, but you should know at least the salary range the school will offer you.

Your last step before your visit is to put together a list of the resources you would need to conduct research and teach classes. Faculty members will ask you many of the same questions that they did during the conference interview, but they will get more specific about money. Create a sample budget that includes equipment you need to set up a lab, copying costs, money for books and conference participation, and so on. If you're not sure what to include, talk with junior faculty in your department to get an idea of their annual expenses. They will have done the same budget projections when they interviewed for jobs.

UNDER THE MICROSCOPE

The biggest difference between the conference interview and the campus visit is social. By this point your qualifications are obviously suited to the department's expectations. They don't need to know, "Are you qualified?" but rather, "Are you someone we want to have lunch with?" The campus interview is a chance for you to demonstrate your fit with the department culture.

It's important to emphasize your people skills as well as your academic expertise. You can be more personable in this interview than the last. That's what the faculty are looking for, and one of the reasons your visit includes receptions, parties, and other social gatherings.

LAST ROUND

You'll have at least one more interview with the faculty, which may also include members of the university administration. In addition to a repetition of the questions you've already been asked, they'll want you to ask a few questions. Now that you're getting down to the nitty-gritty details of a possible job, you may want to find out more specific information about your prospective job. Here's a sample from Anthony and Roe's guide:

- What kinds of facilities are available for research? (Be sure to mention any facilities you've come across during your research.)
- What administrative help can I expect from the departmental staff?
- What about funding for conferences and professional development?
- How helpful is the research office in preparing grant proposals?
- What is a typical undergrad class size and composition of the students?
- What kinds of benefits are included in the compensation package?
- Will the department help out with moving expenses?
- When and how will I be notified about this position?

TALK MONEY?

If you're interviewing at more than one school, I think it's okay to talk money. Not only that, but I think you

Try to learn about the personal as well as the professional lives of the faculty. You should be interviewing them as much as they are interviewing you. Remember that a good fit includes more than just an amicable working relationship.

THE WRITING ON THE WALL

Students rarely see the potential opportunities in temporary employment because academics continue to regard temporary employment as a means to an end. That end, the permanent job, is diminishing rapidly, with little or no chance for revival.

Right now, there are only two truly "permanent" jobs in the United States—Supreme Court Justice and tenured professor. The job permanence of the former is guaranteed by the Constitution; nothing guarantees the permanence of the latter!

should let the school know you're interviewing elsewhere. If the faculty knows you're in demand, you may be able to secure a better compensation package. If you only have one interview lined up, you may want the job badly enough that you're not as interested in the pay. The Faculty Salaries Database will give you a general idea of the salary range, so if you get timid, at least you know you're not interviewing in the dark.

THANK-YOU NOTES REVISITED

As with any interview, corporate or academic, thank-you notes are not required but they are appreciated. A polite and personalized thank you is never a waste of time. Take the extra effort to thank faculty for your visit, tell them what a great time you had, and express your continued interest in the job. It keeps your name in their heads. Even if you don't get the job, these faculty will remember you fondly when you're off doing research elsewhere. They will continue to be valuable contacts, no matter where you end up.

THE MYTH OF THE "PERMANENT" JOB

I am not surprised when I hear angry stories from students about how little their education has prepared them for the realities of employment. Many students right now feel betrayed—by their advisers, by the administration, by the "system"—for continuing to enroll graduate students who can't be placed in permanent jobs. And this hostility is justified, especially in response to faculty members who shrug their shoulders and sympathize without offering concrete alternatives.

But before dashing off a scathing article to *Lingua Franca*, let's take a look at the employment sphere beyond academe. Downsizing and restructuring have been going on longer in nonacademic environments, and the results suggest that the "permanent" job is becoming a thing of the past, a holdover from the expectations of earlier generations. Remember when your parents described the rewards of working at a company for 20 or 30 years, a work model that you no doubt resisted? Well, that doesn't happen anymore. If you feel betrayed, just imagine the bewilderment your parents' generation is experiencing about the lack of job security. You've heard stories of employees who give 15 years to a company, only to be cut loose and replaced with outsourcing, consultants, and part-time contractors. Like you, these employees did all the right things, followed the rules, and still got laid off. As a result, many nonacademic employees view this changing employment trend as an ominous threat to the status quo.

And academics are not immune to this negative attitude. Many continue to regard academic "temping" as a dirty word. This attitude influences grad students. In the humanities, students worry that they will get stuck in "Adjunct Hell" or become "Gypsy Scholars," constantly on the move from one short-term appointment to the next. The same anxiety crosses over to the sciences, where students fear they will get stuck in "Post-Doc Purgatory" and never land a permanent job.

EMBRACING THE POST-INDUSTRIAL AGE

What I want to offer here is a radically new vision—a positive vision—of this dynamic economic environment. And this vision includes you. In a postindustrial labor market, information is the new wave of demand. The Information Age requires the skill of "knowledge workers"—independent and educated people who provide their expertise for pay. As a graduate student, this changing market may be right up your alley. What employers seek are manipulators of information—consultants who can offer their brainpower to solve a given problem, then move on to the next problem, whether it's with a different team or a different company. And this is exactly what you've spent your graduate career doing: finding, analyzing, and disseminating information to solve problems.

This changing employment vision means incredible opportunity for graduate students. The restructuring of the work environment may be particularly suited to your skills and personality. Unlike older academics and nonacademics who expect and need the security of a full-time office environment, you have been taught to work independently and at home.

In this terrible job market, I plan to try for a tenure-track teaching position as long as my funds hold out. If not, then I'll get a "real" job somewhere and not feel cheated or bitter, as some of my fellow grads seem to feel. After all, I got what I came for, a first-rate education in a field I truly love. I'll do my best in the job search and live—joyfully—with the result, because the Ph.D. has opened up new worlds to me.

—June, Ph.D. student, English

THE REALITY OF CONSULTANCY

The "knowledge worker" of the postindustrial economy is usually an independent consultant. Here's how it works. You join an organization for a few years to acquire skills in a particular field. During that time you make contacts inside and outside the organization. You make a name for yourself. Once you've mastered that skill, you go out on your own. Many times you will continue to work on a contract or part-time basis with your former employer. Although at first your overall income is less than before, your hourly rate is substantially higher. At the same time, as a "consultant" you begin to take on other clients through your established networks. Word gets around. More clients seek out your services. You partner with other consultants to get more contacts and take on larger projects. Your hourly rate and your billable hours increase. After a few years the independent home office has expanded to include an outside office and administrative support. Eventually the consultancy becomes a business in its own right.

I've seen this happen to friends and colleagues more times than I can count. I've read about ex-employees who strike out on their own and get offered stock options instead of high salaries from start-up companies. Sometimes these options pay off far beyond their expectations.

I've yet to meet a successful consultant who ever wants to go back into the office again. They enjoy "sitting in their underwear" while conducting business, having more time to spend at home with their children, playing music or having the TV on while they're working. They feel more connected to their local communities than ever before. And no one misses traffic congestion!

The emergence of the flexible, Information-Age "personal entrepreneur" offers real career possibilities for students frustrated with the academic employment horizon. If any one group is suited to the demands of this changing economy, it is the grad student community. Grad students come prepackaged with the skills necessary to be successful consultants, the providers of sought-after information services. No matter what industry you choose—even if you decide to stay in education or an education-related administrative job—

this new model can work for you. While you're finishing up your degree, expand your vision to include career opportunities that take advantage of this shifting economic paradigm. Redefine your goals in a way that applies your analytical skills to your own future as well as your academic pursuits. If you do, you will prosper, no matter what career path you choose.

I am currently a full-time professional staff member at my university as a teaching consultant. I'd like to continue in this kind of job, although I'd also like the chance to teach an occasional course. I began grad school twelve years ago wanting to be a "scholar"; I realized that teaching, and talking about teaching, was much more fun.

—Rick, Ph.D graduate, English

OTHER GOOD BOOKS

Allison, Alida, and Terri Frongia. *The Grad Student's Guide to Getting Published.* New York: Prentice Hall, 1992.

The title says it all. This is the only publication of its kind, targeted specifically at grad students rather than junior faculty or established scholars. Covers relationships with students and mentors in finding publication avenues and topics; finding and submitting to the right journals; doing book reviews; finding and submitting to book publishers; and making good use of the library to track down a publisher. Includes tips from librarians, university press editors, journal editors, faculty, and students. The book's only drawback is a lack of information on electronic publishing, but, despite this weakness, it's an essential guide for any grad student who heeds the call of "publish or perish."

Anthony, Rebecca, and Gerald Roe. *Finding a Job in Your Field: A Handbook for Ph.D.'s and M.A.'s.* Princeton: Peterson's Guides, 1984.

Despite its age, this book is still the best source available on the academic job search. University hiring procedures for tenure-track jobs haven't changed much over the last twelve years. Offers a great sampling of CVs and resumes covering several fields, along with samples of different kinds of letters—letter of inquiry, letter of application, letter following the interview, and so on. Also includes a detailed overview of the process of academic interviewing.

Benjaminson, Peter. *Publish Without Perishing: A Practical Handbook for Academic Authors.* Washington: NEA Professional Library, 1992. (A Joint Project of the National Education Association and the National Writers Union.)

The other sources listed here are more appropriate to grad student authors, but I included this book for one very important reason: the information on book contracts. I didn't find another source that offered the same level of detailed and comprehensive information on contracts for academic authors. Covers the ins and outs of advances and royalties, copyright, subsidiary rights, contract negotiations, and reprints. Check this source before you sign a contract with a book publisher.

Cheshire, Barbara W. *The Best Dissertation . . . A Finished Dissertation.* Portland: National Book Company, 1993.

Written in an informal and entertaining style, this book is also short enough to be read in one sitting. Its best feature is a step-by-step outline for organizing and writing each chapter of the dissertation. Cheshire also offers several tips on writing.

Groneman, Carol, and Robert N. Lear. *Corporate PhD: Making the Grade in Business.* New York: Facts on File, 1985.

For those students seeking alternatives to tenure-track employment, this is the book for you. The authors provide seven detailed case studies of Ph.D.s who left academe to pursue nonacademic careers. The case studies are fascinating reading: Ph.D. grads describe why they left the academy and how they found successful careers in business. No two stories are alike, and each offers different job search strategies for making the transition to the corporate arena. In addition, the authors interviewed employers in a variety of fields, asking them to describe the pros and cons of hiring Ph.D.s in their own organizations. By the time you finish this book, you may be convinced that a nonacademic career is your best option.

Harman, Eleanor, and Ian Montagnes, eds. *The Thesis and the Book.* Toronto: U of Toronto P, 1976.

This is the only book I've included from the disco era. Why? Because no source has yet to supersede it. This is the best book of its kind on turning your thesis/dissertation into a publishable book. Especially helpful is the contribution by Olive Holmes, "Thesis to book: what to get rid of" and "what to do with what is left." Everything that is said about the "dissertation don'ts" still applies in the 1990s. If you want to get your thesis/dissertation published, read this short guide before you get started.

Hawley, Peggy. *Being Bright is Not Enough: The Unwritten Rules of Doctoral Study.* Springfield: Charles C. Thomas, 1993.

Hawley's book focuses on the social sciences, in terms of data gathering, but this source is useful to all Ph.D. students in selecting an adviser and committee, preparing the dissertation proposal, and gearing up for the oral defense. Unlike most dissertation guides, Hawley includes engaging feedback and stories from other students. Her last chapter on spouses, families, and friends contains the only information I've seen on balancing the conflicting demands of social life and grad school. Wish it had been longer!

Locke, Lawrence F., Waneen Wyrick Spirduso, and Stephen J. Silverman. *Proposals That Work: A Guide for Planning Dissertations and Grant Proposals.* 3rd ed. Newbury Park, CA: Sage Publications, 1993.

This guide includes helpful sample proposals of an experimental study, qualitative study, a quasi-experimental design proposal, and a funded grant proposal. It also contains an annotated bibliography of supplementary references. A little dense at times, but very helpful to science and social science students. In addition, this guide offers a chapter on preparing qualitative research proposals, which most grant and dissertation guides do not cover.

Luey, Beth. *Handbook for Academic Authors.* 3rd ed. Cambridge: Cambridge UP, 1995.

This book has just been reissued in a third edition, and I can see why it continues to be successful. Although targeted at junior faculty, it includes relevant information for grad students in each chapter. Luey covers topics such as submitting journal articles, revising the dissertation, and finding book publishers—including textbooks, multiauthor works, and anthologies. The book also provides useful information on the mechanics of production, editing, permissions, and contract negotiations, and includes sample permission request forms.

Madson, David. *Successful Dissertations and Theses.* San Francisco: Jossey-Bass Publishers, 1983.

Madson's guide is targeted at students in the social and behavioral sciences. It covers working with an adviser and committee, selecting a topic, and preparing the research proposal. Also includes a chapter on publishing and presenting the thesis/dissertation. His appendix offers useful sample proposals from historical and experimental approaches.

McKeachie, Wilbert James. *Teaching Tips: A Guidebook for the Beginning College Teacher.* 8th ed. Lexington, MA: D. C. Heath, 1986.

For schools that do not offer a TA training manual (and even for some of those that do), McKeachie's guidebook serves as the "TA Bible." For students who know that teaching will be a significant part of their graduate education, I even recommend buying this book—you'll never need any other source to prepare you for teaching undergrads. Covers everything from university policies and procedures to developing a course schedule and syllabi to tips on lecturing and discussion approaches in the classroom.

McWade, Patricia. *Financing Graduate School: How to Get the Money You Need for Your Graduate School Education,* 2nd ed. Princeton: Peterson's Guides, 1996.

Your one-stop shopping guide to graduate financial aid. This book offers comprehensive information on graduate financial aid, concentrating on federal aid and eligibility guidelines. McWade also includes helpful information on getting grant money and drafting a proposal. The appendices cover general info on grad aid; aid for minorities; aid for women; aid for study abroad; aid for international students; state student scholarship agencies; state student loan guarantee agencies; and professional associations.

Moxley, Joseph M. *Publish, Don't Perish: The Scholar's Guide to Academic Writing and Publishing.* Westport, CT: Greenwood Press, 1992.

I included Moxley's guide in this bibliography because, although Moxley covers many of the same topics on publishing as other books listed here, he covers them from the science and social science perspective. Particularly helpful to students in these areas are his chapters on developing and writing a research notebook, abstracts, and qualitative and quantitative research reports. He also includes a chapter on writing grant proposals. His selected bibliography offers a great list of directories and guides for publishing on particular subjects such as education, health and medicine, technology and science, and the humanities.

Nyquist, Jody D., Robert D. Abbott, Donald H. Wulff, and Jo Sprague, eds. *Preparing the Professoriate of Tomorrow To Teach: Selected Readings in TA Training.* Dubuque, Iowa: Kendall/Hunt, 1991.
This book outlines the steps for building successful TA training programs, including a section on cultural diversity. The essays are written by representatives of different schools who cover detailed aspects of their individual TA training programs. The best feature of this collection is its comprehensive coverage of discipline-specific programs.

Peters, Robert L. *Getting What You Came For: The Smart Student's Guide To Earning a Master's or a Ph.D.* New York: The Noonday Press (Farrar, Straus & Giroux), 1992.
Written by a Ph.D. grad in biology, Peters's book begins with 'why to go' and ends with job hunting. Peters devotes six chapters alone to the thesis/dissertation and includes some great advice on playing departmental politics. Especially helpful is his information on dealing with the social and psychological challenges of grad school, including his chapter on the specific challenges of returning students, women, minorities, and foreign students. His job search chapter is weaker, targeted at getting a nonacademic rather than an academic job, but overall Peters provides a useful and comprehensive guide to grad school.

Ries, Joanne B., and Carl G. Leukefeld. *Applying for Research Funding: Getting Started and Getting Funded.* Thousand Oaks, CA: Sage Publications, 1995.
I thought this was an excellent source for the first-time grant writer who's preparing scientific research proposals. The book takes you through each stage of the proposal writing process and includes

info on laying out a research plan before you begin working on a grant proposal. Also covers writing strategies; timetables; budgeting; and building relationships within both the academic and the grants community.

Rubin, Mary, and the Business and Professional Women's Foundation. *How to Get Money for Research.* Old Westbury, NY: Feminist Press, 1983.
Despite being an older publication, this source provides an excellent annotated bibliography of grant and foundation directories. It's slanted toward money for women but useful to anyone just beginning to search for granting agencies.

Rudestam, Kjell Erik and Rae R. Newton. *Surviving Your Dissertation: A Comprehensive Guide to Content and Process.* Newbury Park, CA: Sage Publications, 1992.
Sage publishes a special series devoted to issues in graduate education, and this is one of their products. Admirably covers the nuts and bolts of dissertation planning and writing, including up-to-date information on computer use. Unfortunately, information on working with the thesis/dissertation committee is brief (two pages), and the book does not include information on selecting an adviser and committee. It does, however, contain a helpful discussion on using a qualitative vs. a quantitative approach to the thesis/dissertation.

Sherrill, Jan-Mitchell and Craig A. Hardesty. *The Gay, Lesbian, and Bisexual Students' Guide to Colleges, Universities, and Graduate Schools.* New York: New York UP, 1994.
This recently published guide surveys 1,464 students, including graduate and professional students, at 189 colleges and universities. The survey asks students to describe their school's position on g/l/b issues, including counseling available to g/l/b students; housing availability for cohabitating students; whether homophobia is a problem on campus and if the school takes action against hate crimes; if the students would have chosen a different school if they'd known about campus climate for g/l/b stu-

dents; university course offerings on g/l/b issues; and if the students would recommend their school to other g/l/b students.

Smith, Robert V. *Graduate Research: A Guide for Students in the Sciences.* Philadelphia: ISI Press, 1984.
Excellent primer for science students. Smith's comprehensive coverage begins with an overview of scientific research, then details the research skills grad students need to develop. The guide includes info on preparing a thesis/dissertation; presenting and publishing papers/posters; conducting research with human subjects, animals, and biohazards; getting grant support; and searching for a job.

Stelzer, Richard J. *How to Write a Winning Personal Statement for Graduate and Professional School.* Princeton: Peterson's, 1989.
Stelzer's book focuses more on professional school admission than grad school, but he offers fifteen samples of successful grad admission essays, plus information from representatives of top graduate and professional schools about what they look for in admission essays. His introduction offers tips on organizing and writing your admissions statement, including self evaluation. Appendix includes different questionnaires for family, friends, and professors to use in evaluating the strengths and weaknesses of your personal statement.

Sternberg, David. *How to Complete and Survive a Doctoral Dissertation.* New York: St. Martin's Press, 1981.
One of my favorites of the thesis/dissertation guides. General enough to be consulted by students in a variety of fields, Sternberg's guide is also engaging and fun to read. He spends less time on components of the proposal and thesis/dissertation itself and addresses more of the psychological stumbling blocks and how to get past them. The book also contains very helpful tips on selecting and working with your adviser and committee.

Thyer, Bruce A. *Successful Publishing in Scholarly Journals.* Thousand Oaks, CA: Sage Publications, 1994.
This recent book on journal publishing offers up-to-date info for both grad students and junior faculty. It

covers much of the same territory as *The Grad Student's Guide to Getting Published*, but offers more detail on the process of journal submissions. Perhaps the best contributions are the chapters on "Marketing Your Published Article" and "Developing a Personal Program of Productive Publishing" (alliterative but quite helpful!).

Walters, Charles. *How to Apply to Graduate School Without Really Lying.* Chicago: Nelson-Hall, 1980.
Walters offers his experiences and "insider info" as a professor who's been involved in the graduate admissions process for a number of years. Humorous and fun to read, this book offers info about the admissions process within the department, specifically selection criteria. Walters offers suggestions on how to be "different" in your essay to catch the eyes of profs. He also suggests ways to evaluate your own ranking when shopping for a school and the best approach for soliciting recommendations. The book also contains a helpful bibliography of grad school directories; indexes of periodical search sources; directories for finding faculty names (bios, location, who's who); financial aid information; prep books for GRE; and job search sources.

INDEX

Costs. *See* Economics; Financial aid

Counseling
  on applications, at undergraduate institution, 22
  for thesis/dissertation, 141–42

Courses
  GRE preparation, 29–30
  language, 77
  for nonacademic employment, 180
  statistics and programming, 135
  work in, 71–83
  teaching and, 88–90

Cover letters for job applications, 187

Cracking the GRE, 29

Credentials for admission, 24

Curriculum vitae (CV), 34
  of professors, 66
  sample, 35–36

D

Data analysis and representation, for thesis/dissertation, 135

Databases, in application research, 19–22

Defense of ideas, 143–44

Defense of thesis/dissertation, 147–50
  failure, 150–51

Departments (academic)
  chairs, in conflict resolution, 147
  climate, as application factor, 15
  guidelines for adviser/committee selection, 132
  interests of, as application factor, 13–14
  placement record, 181
  politics in, 72
  staff, meeting, 63–64

Directories, in application research, 16–18

Directory of Graduate Programs, 16–18

Directory of Research Grants, 47, 117

Discussion groups, 21, 94

Dissertations. *See* Theses and dissertations

Doctorate degree. *See also* Theses and dissertations
  deciding on M.A./M.S. vs., 10–11
  financial aid awards and, 44–45
  nonacademic employment and, 175–76
  time required for, 14

Documentation
  of committee meetings, 143
  in journal articles, 168–69

Dress code
  for campus visit, 41–42
  for conferences, 160

E

Economics
  graduate school downsizing/restructuring, 8–9
  grants to university, 15
  job market, 174–75, 192–93
  nonacademic employment, 104–5
  travel expenses for conferences, 159–60

The Educational Rankings Annual, 18

Educational Testing Service
  Directory of Graduate Programs, 16–18
  prep guide, 32

Electronic publishing, 173

E-mail, 67, 107, 114

Employment. *See* Jobs; Job search

Engineering fellowships, 50

Entrepreneurialism, 194–95

Environment, departmental, as application factor, 15

ERA, 18

Essays (statement of purpose), 38–41

ETS
  Directory of Graduate Programs, 16–18
  prep guide, 32

Examinations, 71–83. *See also* Graduate Record Examinations
  committee, 75
  failure, 83
  foreign language, 77
  given by teaching assistants, 91, 96–97
  grading, 76
  length, 75
  at M.A./M.S. and Ph.D. levels, 3
  mock, 81–82
  preparation, 75–76, 78–83
  types, 76–77

Exercise, 101–2

F

Facilities, special, 15

Faculty
  interests of, as application factor, 13–14
  interviewing, 66–68
  intimate relationships with, 146
  meeting, 64
  research on, 19–20, 65

Faculty advisers, 4–5, 68
  problems and solutions with, 145–47
  relations with, 142–45
  selecting, 131–33

Faculty Salaries Database, 190

FAFSA, 56

Failure
  on examinations, 83
  on oral defense of thesis/dissertation, 150–51

Family, 102–4

Federal aid, application for, 56–57

Federal Direct Student Loans, 57

Fellowships, 48–50
  publications on, 15–16

Field of study, selection of, 12

Financial aid, 43–58
  as application factor, 13
  applying for, 44
  assistantships, 45–47
  for conferences, 158–59

J

Jacob K. Javits Graduate Fellowships, 49
Jobs
    changing environment, 193–95
    consultancy, 194–95
    declining market, 174–75
    for graduates, as application factor, 14
    impermanence of, 192–93
    networking and, 106
    nonacademic, 104–5, 175–76
    placement, 65–66
Job search, 174–95
    academic, 186
      cover letter, 187
      interviews, 187–92
      resources, 186–87
      salaries, 190, 191–92
      thank-you notes, 192
    nonacademic
      classes, 180
      informational interviews, 182–85
      internships, 180
      networking, 180–82
      offer of employment, 185
      on-line and library resources, 178–80
      skills inventory, 176–78
      strategy, 185
Jobtrack, 179
Journal articles. *See also* Publishing
    based on class paper or thesis/dissertation, 167–69
    as idea source, 130–31
    Internet and, 106
Journals
    assessing, 163
    peer-reviewed, 164
    prestige of, 167

K

Kaplan GRE prep course, 29–30
Key words in literature search, 111–12

L

Laboratories, visiting, 68
Laboratory sessions, conducted by teaching assistants, 92
Language examinations, 77
Lear, Robert N., 184
Lecturing, 92–93
Libraries
    effective searching in, 111
    in job search, 179–80
    research in, for applications, 16–20
    tour of, 69
Literature search/review, 111
    excessive, 141
    for grant proposal, 119–20
Loans, 54–57
Location of school, as application factor, 14–15

M

Master's degree. *See also* Theses and dissertations
    deciding on Ph.D. vs., 10–11
    financial aid awards and, 44–45
Meetings with adviser, 143
Mellon Fellowships, 49–50
Mentors, 5
Minorities, financial aid for, 53–54
Mock examinations, 81–82
M.S. *See* Master's degree
Multiple submissions
    of articles, 164–65
    to university presses, 172

N

National Defense Science and Engineering Graduate Fellowship Program, 50
National Endowment for the Humanities annual report, 19
National Science Foundation
    annual report, 19
    Graduate Research Fellowships, 50
    Minority Graduate Fellowships, 54
Nelson, Cary, 175
Networking, 59, 61, 105–7
    for nonacademic jobs, 180–82
Notes

in examination preparation, 79–80
    for research, 111
    for thesis/dissertation, 137

O

Office of Naval Research Graduate Fellowship Program, 50
On-line publications, 21–22
On-line resources for job search, 178–79
Oral defense of thesis/dissertation, 147–50
    failure, 150–51
Oral examinations, videotape in preparation for, 82
Organization
    for research, 100
    for thesis/dissertation, 137–39
Orientation, 59–70
    independent, 60, 62–66
    obtaining information, 60–62
    university programs, 62

P

Papers, scholarly. *See* Journal articles; Publishing
Parents, 103–4
Part-time education, full-time education vs., 11
Patricia Roberts Harris Fellowship, 54
Peer review
    of books, 172
    of journal articles, 164
Periodicals. *See* Journals
Perkins loans, 55–56
Personality conflicts, 145
Personal statement, in application, 38–41
Peters, Robert L., 58, 79
Peterson's Guide to Graduate and Professional Programs, 16–17
Ph.D. *See* Doctorate degree
Phones, 115
Pilot study for thesis/dissertation, 135
Politics, 2, 72, 108–9
Printed materials, in application research, 16–19

Professors. *See* Faculty
Programming courses, for thesis/dissertation, 135
Proposals
   for grants, 116–24
   for theses/dissertations, 134–37
Psychological strategies for thesis/dissertation, 139–41
Publications, as idea source, 130–31
Publishing, 162–73. *See also* Journal articles; Journals
   articles based on thesis/dissertation, 167–69
   book reviews, 169–70
   electronic, 173
   finding appropriate journal, 163
   formats for articles, 169
   Internet and, 106
   multiple submissions, 164–65
   peer-reviewed journals, 164
   prestige of journal, 167
   readers and staff, 164
   reader's report, 165, 166
   rejection, 166
   revision and resubmission, 165
   in unviversity press, 170–72
   when to submit papers, 162–63

Q
Queries to publishers, 171–72
Questions
   from faculty on thesis/dissertation, 149–50
   how to ask, 93–94
   at interviews
      for academic jobs, 188–91
      for nonacademic jobs, 183–84
   after paper presentation, 161–62
Quiet students, 94–95

R
Rank of school
   as application factor, 15–16

publications on, 18
RA's, 104
Recommendation letters
   collecting, 38
   information provided to writers of, 34, 37
Relationships with professors, 146
Relaxation, 142
Requirements
   academic program, 71–73
   foreign language, 77–78
   thesis, 127
Research, 99–124
   in academic job search, 186–87, 190
   grant proposals, 116–24
   interdisciplinary, 11–12
   literature review, 119–22
   networking and, 105–7
   organization for, 100
   scheduling time, 101–5
   in selecting university
      strategies, 12–16
      tools, 16–22
   socialization and politics, 107–9
   techniques, 110
   for thesis or dissertation, 3–4
   time-saving strategies, 110–14
   time wasters, 114–15
   topic selection, 118–19
Research assistants, 104
Research assistantships, 45–46
Research Office, 116
Research university, teaching university vs., 10
Residence Hall Director, 50–51
Roe, Gerald, 181, 188, 189
Role-playing
   in classroom, 94
   for conference presentations, 161
Rubin, Mary, 123

S
Salaries, in academic jobs, 190, 191–92
Scholarships, 51–52
Science Citation Index, 20

Sciences
   fellowships, 50
   specialization and, 2
   theses and dissertations in, 4
Selection of field of study, 12
Selection of university, 7–23
   author's experience, 7–8
   considerations before application, 10–12
   Internet and, 20–22
   paring down list, 23
   research strategies, 12–16
   research tools, 16–20
   undergraduate institutional assistance, 22
Self-doubt, 139–40
Self-promotion, 40
Skills inventory, in job search, 176–78
Slides, for conference presentations, 160–61
Social life, research and, 102, 107–9
Social Sciences Citation Index, 20
Social sciences fellowships, 49
Specialization, 1, 2, 5
Speech, in oral examinations, 82–83
Speed-reading, 112–13
Stafford loans, 55–56
Statement of purpose, 38–41
Statistics courses, for thesis/dissertation, 135
Sternberg, David, 149, 150
Study groups, 80–81
Study guides for GRE's, 29
Subject Test of GRE, 28, 32, 33
Support, 107, 142
Syllabus, of teaching assistants, 89, 91

T
Talkative students, 95
TA's. *See* Teaching assistants
Teaching, 5, 84–98
   balancing course work and, 88
   balancing research and, 104

GRE* Success
Three full-length GRE tests with explanatory answers. Includes preparing for the GRE on computer.
ISBN 688-x (with disk), 448 pp., 8 1/2 x 11, $24.95 pb
ISBN 686-3 (without disk), $12.95 pb

GMAT* Success
Two simulated tests and diagnostic exercises. Includes test-prep strategies.
ISBN 608-1 (with disk), 352 pp., 8 1/2 x 11, $24.95 pb
ISBN 583-2, (without disk), $12.95 pb

LSAT* Success
Three simulated LSATs, 1- to 7-week study programs, and strategies for dealing with test anxiety.
ISBN 609-X (with disk), 352 pp., 8 1/2 x 11, $24.95 pb, 2nd edition
ISBN 585-9 (without disk), $12.95 pb

MCAT Success
Three full-length tests—with answers. Plus—reviews verbal, writing, and graphic sections.
ISBN 689-8 (with disk), 576 pp., 8 1/2 x 11, $24.95 pb
ISBN 685-5 (without disk), $12.95 pb

Guide to MBA Programs 1997
Profiles 700 U.S., Canadian, and international programs.
ISBN 643-X, 1,002 pp., 8 1/2 x 11, $21.95 pb, 2nd edition

Guide to Graduate Computer Science and Electrical Engineering Programs
Details on every accredited graduate computer science and electrical engineering program in the U.S. and Canada—nearly 900 of them. Includes tables, charts, indexes, and informative articles.
ISBN 663-4, 900 pp., 8 1/2 x 11, $24.95 pb

How to Write a Winning Personal Statement for Graduate & Professional School
Richard J. Stelzer
Views of admissions officers, 30+ examples of successful statements, important questions, and more.
ISBN 287-6, 150 pp., 6 x 9, $12.95 pb, 2nd edition

Financing Graduate School
Patricia McWade
Covers differences in undergraduate and graduate aid, eligibility, and more.
ISBN 638-3, 202 pp., 6 x 9, $16.95, 2nd edition

ISBN Prefix: 1-56079-

*GRE is a registered trademark of Educational Testing Service, GMAT is a registered trademark of the College Board, and LSAT is a registered trademark of the Law School Admission Services—none of which has any connection with these books.

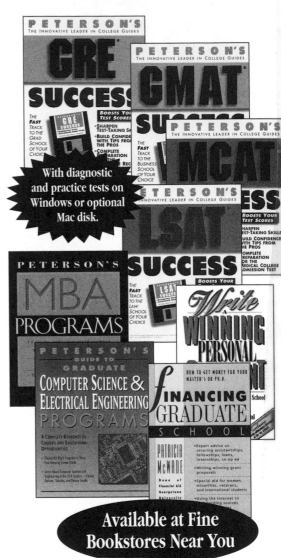

Prepare for Graduate or Professional School Admission with These Peterson's Guides

With diagnostic and practice tests on Windows or optional Mac disk.

Available at Fine Bookstores Near You

Or Order Direct
Call: 800-338-3282   Fax: 609-243-9150

Visit Peterson's Education Center
on the Internet http://www.petersons.com

P **Peterson's** Princeton, NJ